MOTHER,
COME HOME

$(Fx \supset (Gx \ \& \ Hx))$

$\forall x (Fx \supset Gx)$

$\forall x (Fx \supset (Gx \ \& \ Hx))$

$Fa \supset Ga \ \& \ Ha$

STEP

$\forall x$

a

$\sim a \sim$

$\forall x \sim x$

$Fx \ v$

$\exists x (F$

$\exists x \ Fx$

$\exists x (Fx \ v$

$\exists x ($

P

R

R

R

$NY -$

(Gx) $\exists G$ $\exists x$

$\exists x (F$

$x)$

If Mary loves anyone, then she loves John

$(\exists x (Lmx) \supset Lmj)$ OR $\forall x (Lmx \supset Lmj)$

OTHER BOOKS FROM PAUL HORNSCHEMEIER

THE COLLECTED SEQUENTIAL

LET US BE PERFECTLY CLEAR

THE THREE PARADOXES

LIFE WITH MR. DANGEROUS

ALL AND SUNDRY

OTHER BOOKS IN THIS SERIES

JUST OFF TRANSPARENT

THE NEW GLASSES

THE PAPER HIDE

$(Fx \supset (Gx \& Hx)$

$\forall x (Fx \supset Gx)$

STEP

$\forall x \ldots$

$\ldots a$

$\sim a$

$\forall x \sim x$

$x Fx \quad v$

$\exists x (F$

$\exists x Fx$

$\exists x (Fx \ v$

$\exists x ($

$\overline{P}^{(i)} \quad G$

$\dot{R}$

R

$NY -$

$\forall x (Fx \supset (Gx \& Hx))$

$Fa \supset Ga \& Ha$

$(Gx)^{(3)} \exists x \quad \exists x$

$\exists x (F$

MOTHER,
COME HOME

PAUL HORNSCHEMEIER

WITH AN INTRODUCTION BY
THOMAS TENNANT

FANTAGRAPHICS BOOKS, SEATTLE

and a

If Mary loves anyone, then she loves John

$[\exists x Lmx) \supset Lmj$ OR $\forall x (Lmx \supset Lmj)$

Published by
FANTAGRAPHICS BOOKS
7563 Lake City Way NE
Seattle, Washington 98115

Designed by Paul Hornschemeier
Promotion by Eric Reynolds
Collection edited by Diana Schutz
Fantagraphics edition edited by Gary Groth
Published by Gary Groth and Kim Thompson

This volume collects new material along with issues 2-4 of the comic book
series *Forlorn Funnies, Vol. 1*, originally published by Absence of Ink.

Distributed in the U.S. by
W.W. Norton and Company, Inc. (212-354-500)

Distributed in Canada by
the Canadian Manda group (1-416-516-0911)

Distributed in the United Kingdom by
Turnaround Distribution (108-829-3009)

ISBN: 978-1-56097-973-9

First Fantagraphics printing: March, 2009

Printed in Singapore

FOR MY FATHER.
WITH GREATER RESPECT EACH DAY.

MOTHER,
COME HOME

INTRODUCTION
TO THE SECOND EDITION

SECTION ONE:

"OUR MUTUAL DISAPPEARANCE"

INTRODUCTION BY THOMAS TENNANT

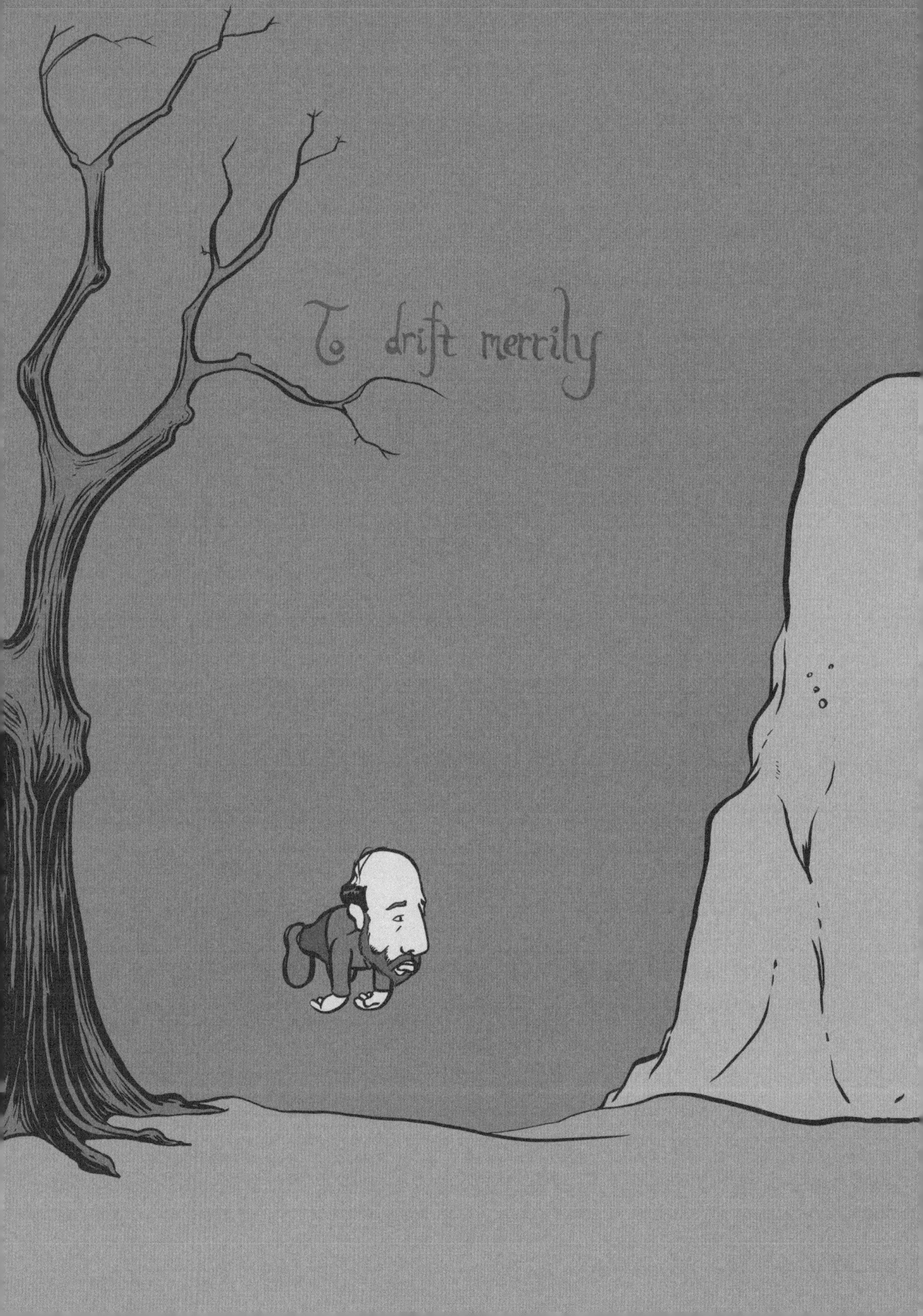
To drift merrily

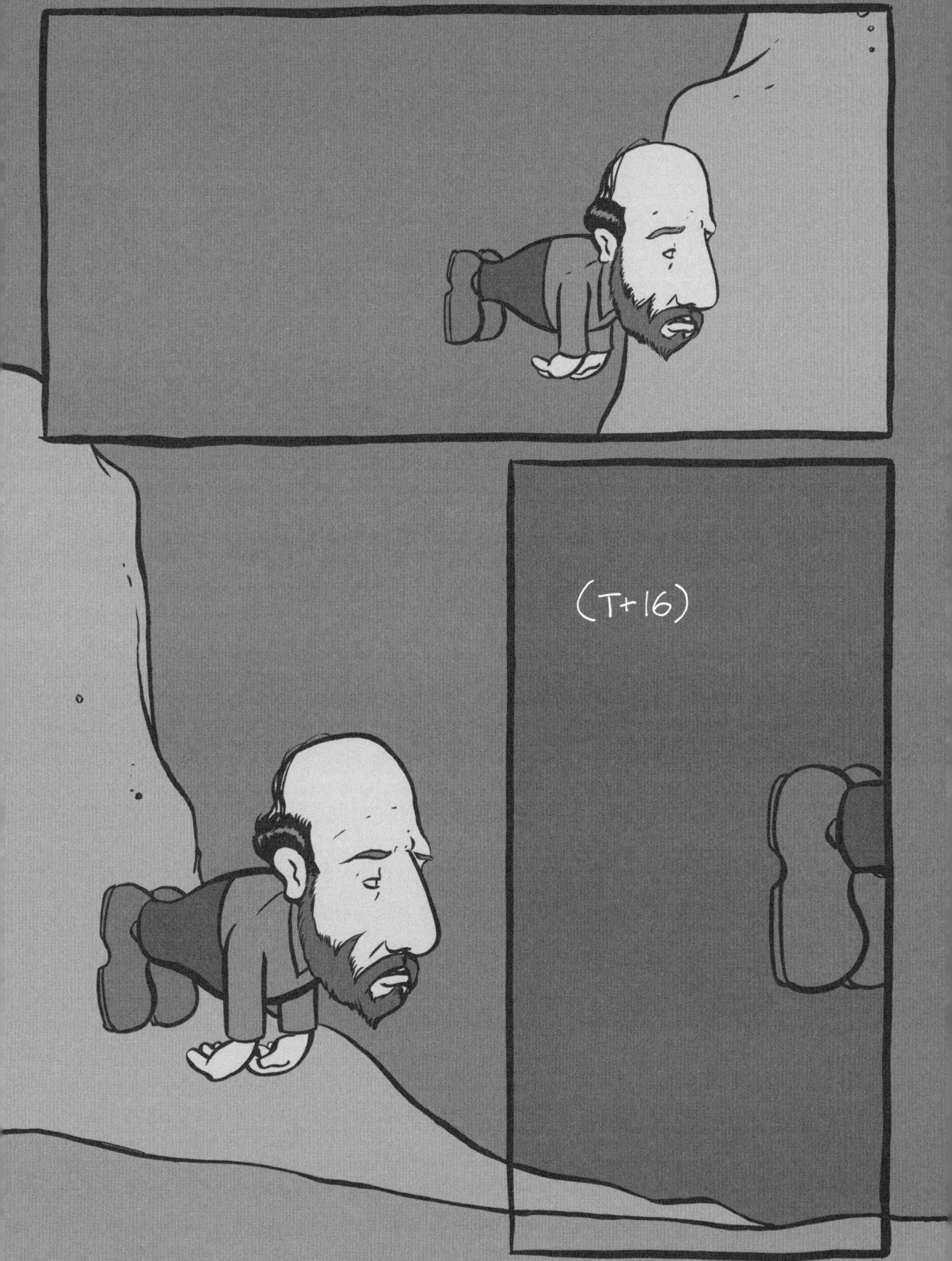
(T+16)

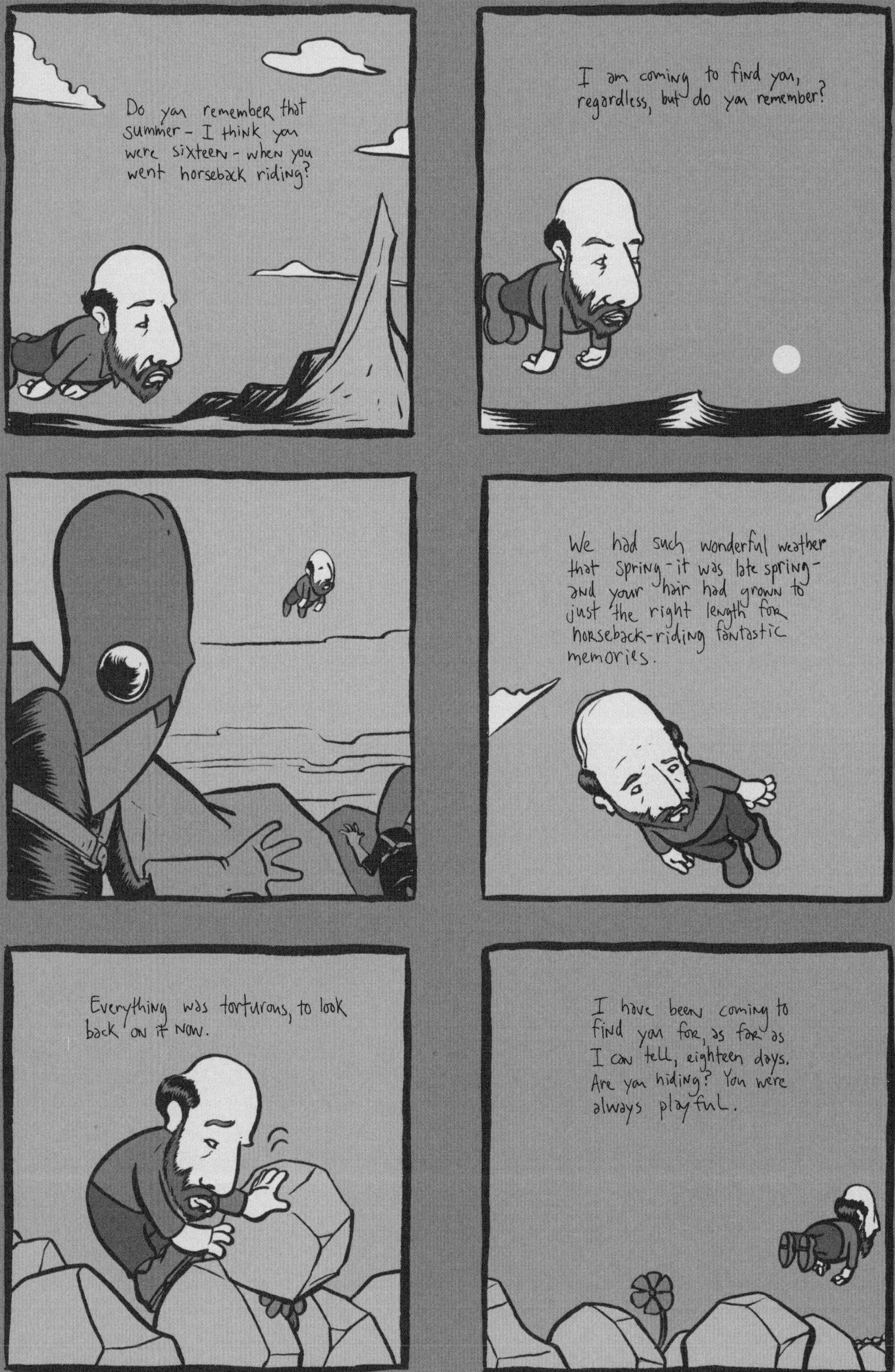
Do you remember that summer – I think you were sixteen – when you went horseback riding?
I am coming to find you, regardless, but do you remember?
We had such wonderful weather that spring – it was late spring – and your hair had grown to just the right length for horseback-riding fantastic memories.
Everything was torturous, to look back on it now.
I have been coming to find you for, as far as I can tell, eighteen days. Are you hiding? You were always playful.

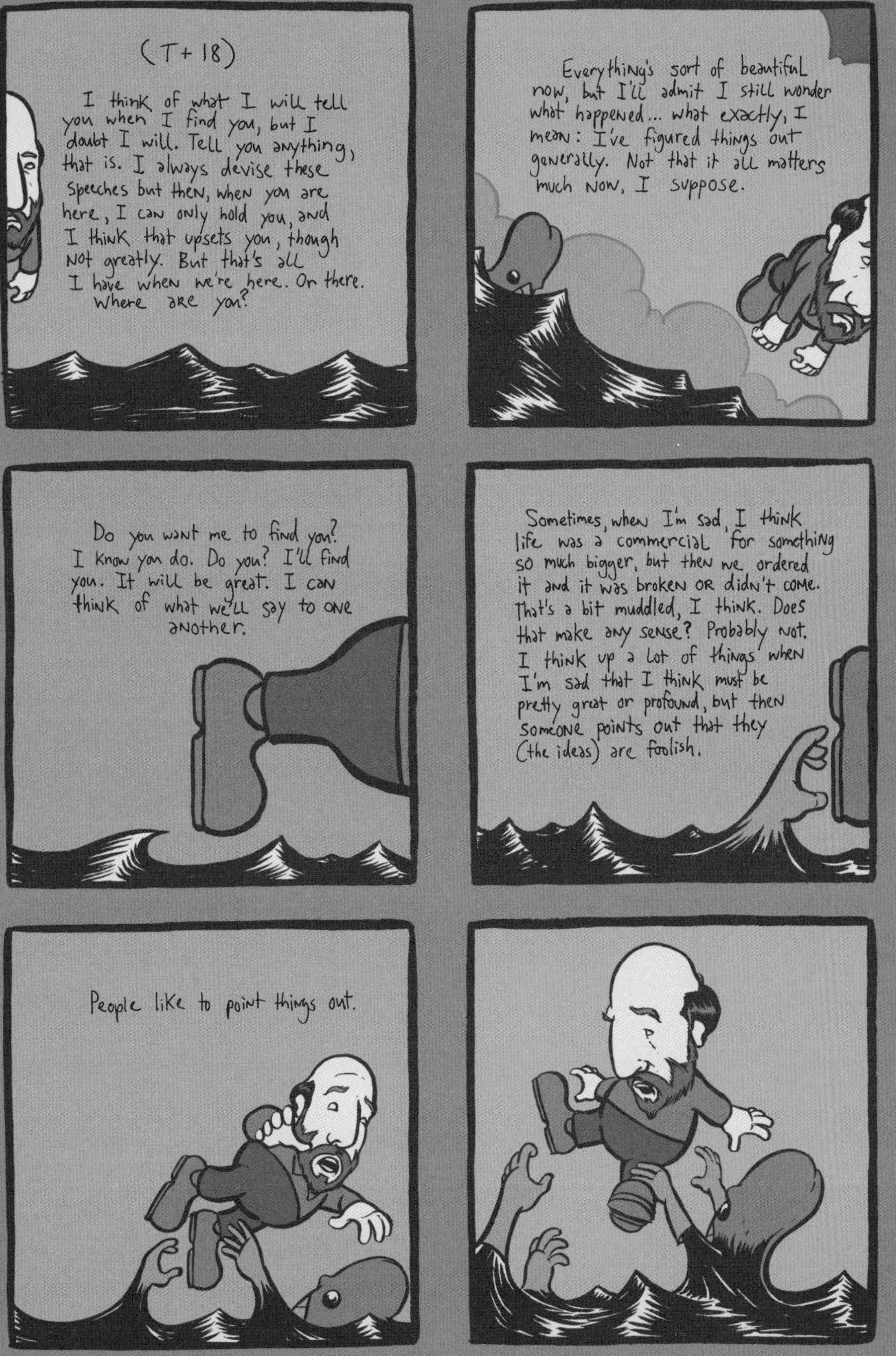
(T+18)
I think of what I will tell you when I find you, but I doubt I will. Tell you anything, that is. I always devise these speeches but then, when you are here, I can only hold you, and I think that upsets you, though not greatly. But that's all I have when we're here. Or there. Where are you?
Everything's sort of beautiful now, but I'll admit I still wonder what happened... what exactly, I mean: I've figured things out generally. Not that it all matters much now, I suppose.
Do you want me to find you? I know you do. Do you? I'll find you. It will be great. I can think of what we'll say to one another.
Sometimes, when I'm sad, I think life was a commercial for something so much bigger, but then we ordered it and it was broken or didn't come. That's a bit muddled, I think. Does that make any sense? Probably not. I think up a lot of things when I'm sad that I think must be pretty great or profound, but then someone points out that they (the ideas) are foolish.
People like to point things out.

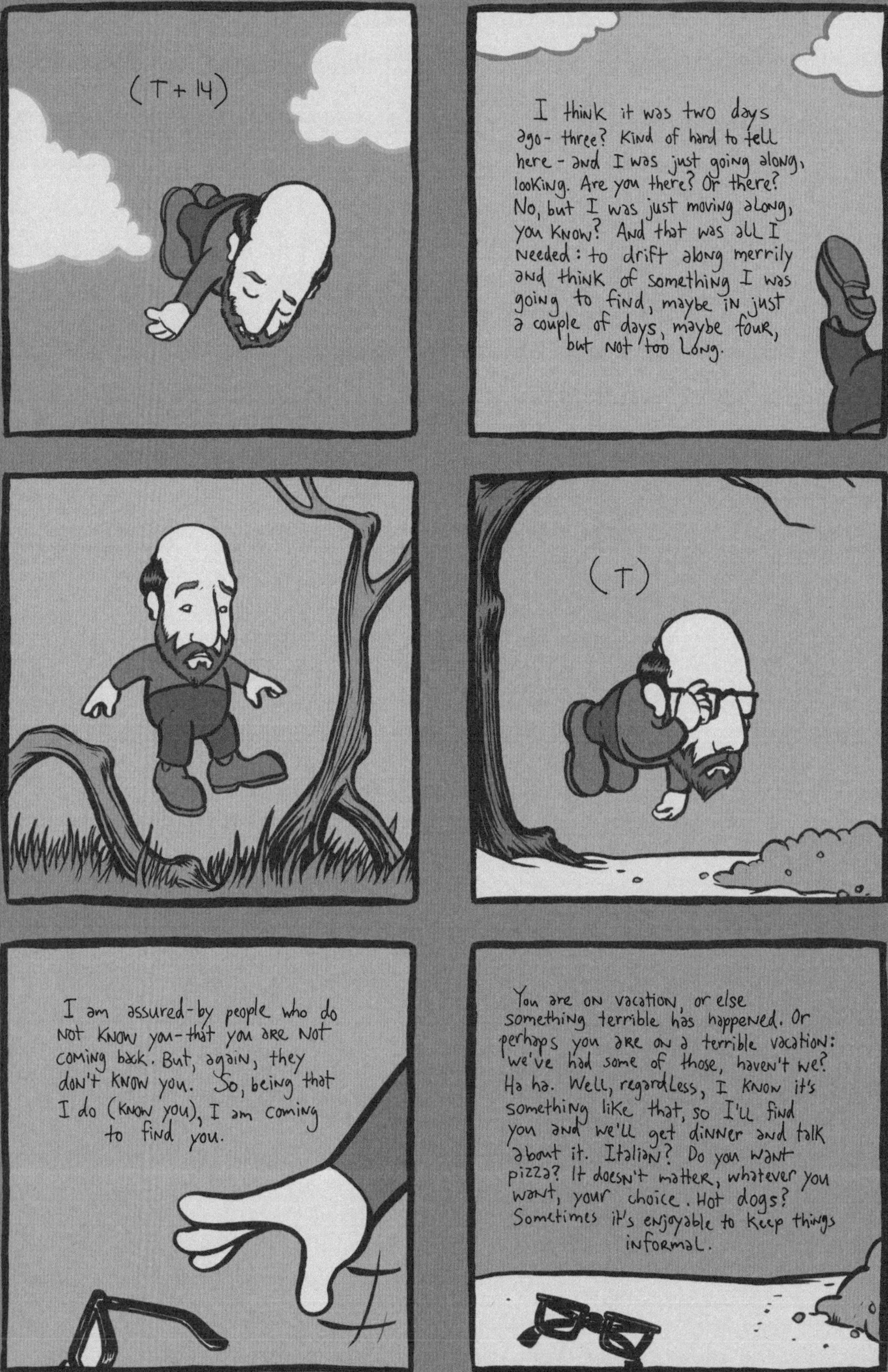
(T + 14)
I think it was two days ago- three? Kind of hard to tell here - and I was just going along, looking. Are you there? Or there? No, but I was just moving along, you know? And that was all I needed: to drift along merrily and think of something I was going to find, maybe in just a couple of days, maybe four, but not too long.
(T)
I am assured-by people who do not know you-that you are not coming back. But, again, they don't know you. So, being that I do (know you), I am coming to find you.
You are on vacation, or else something terrible has happened. Or perhaps you are on a terrible vacation: we've had some of those, haven't we? Ha ha. Well, regardless, I know it's something like that, so I'll find you and we'll get dinner and talk about it. Italian? Do you want pizza? It doesn't matter, whatever you want, your choice. Hot dogs? Sometimes it's enjoyable to keep things informal.

(T + 15)

One thing I think about when I'm in an open space – a space too open to hide you – is that it isn't hot. This is seemingly unremarkable, but I'm not being clear: it's not hot, but it's not _not_ hot. You see? There doesn't seem to be any temperature at all, is my general point. Specifically, I, for some reason, expect it to be hot, but instead feel only a dull neutrality, thermally speaking.

Ultimately though, I recognize the temperature to be a simple distraction. It sways my mood a little bit, but I force myself, for the most part, to ignore it and go about my search.

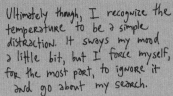

There are multiple distractions that somehow leak themselves in, even into these open spaces. Things about cleaning and creditors. All sorts of ephemera...

Little ghosts to be brushed aside.

There is one that keeps occurring to me though.

Something that I think may be of some import. Something we created together.

A doll? A talking something? Something that made us happy.

I will look for it – WE will look for it – after I find you, but only after. It is important to prioritize.

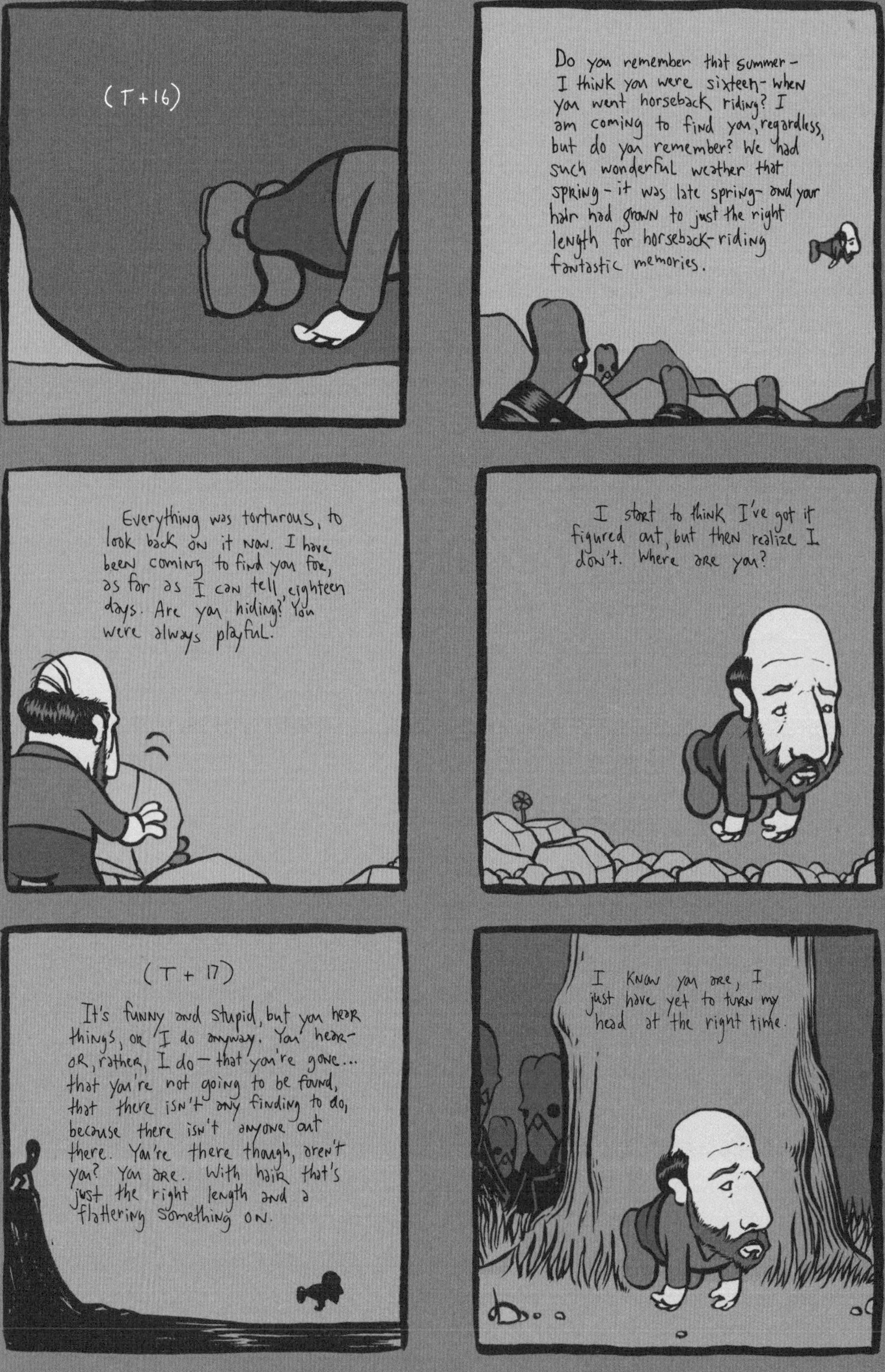
(T+16)
Do you remember that summer— I think you were sixteen— when you went horseback riding? I am coming to find you, regardless, but do you remember? We had such wonderful weather that spring— it was late spring— and your hair had grown to just the right length for horseback-riding fantastic memories.
Everything was torturous, to look back on it now. I have been coming to find you for, as far as I can tell, eighteen days. Are you hiding? You were always playful.
I start to think I've got it figured out, but then realize I don't. Where are you?
(T + 17)
It's funny and stupid, but you hear things, or I do anyway. You hear— or, rather, I do— that you're gone... that you're not going to be found, that there isn't any finding to do, because there isn't anyone out there. You're there though, aren't you? You are. With hair that's just the right length and a flattering something on.
I know you are, I just have yet to turn my head at the right time.

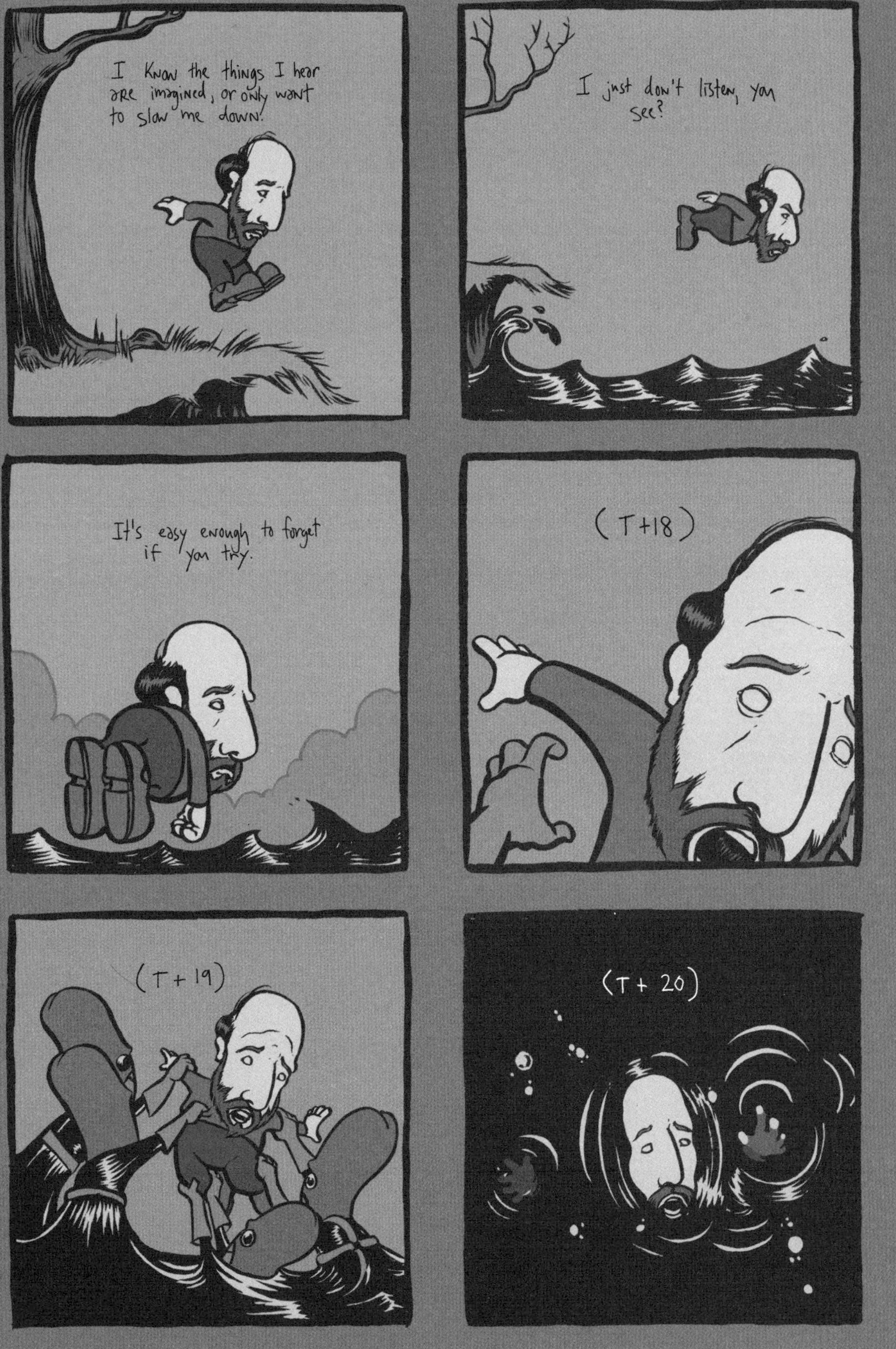
I Know the things I hear are imagined, or only want to slow me down.
I just don't listen, you see?
It's easy enough to forget if you try.
(T+18)
(T+19)
(T+20)

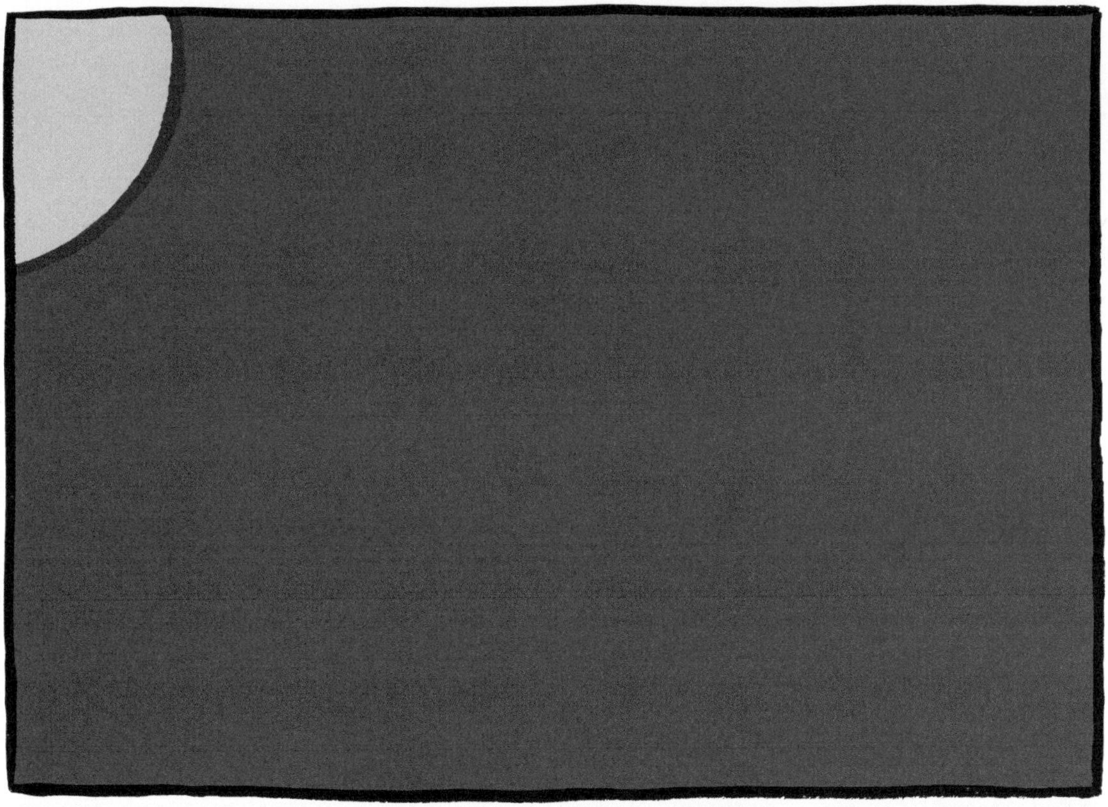
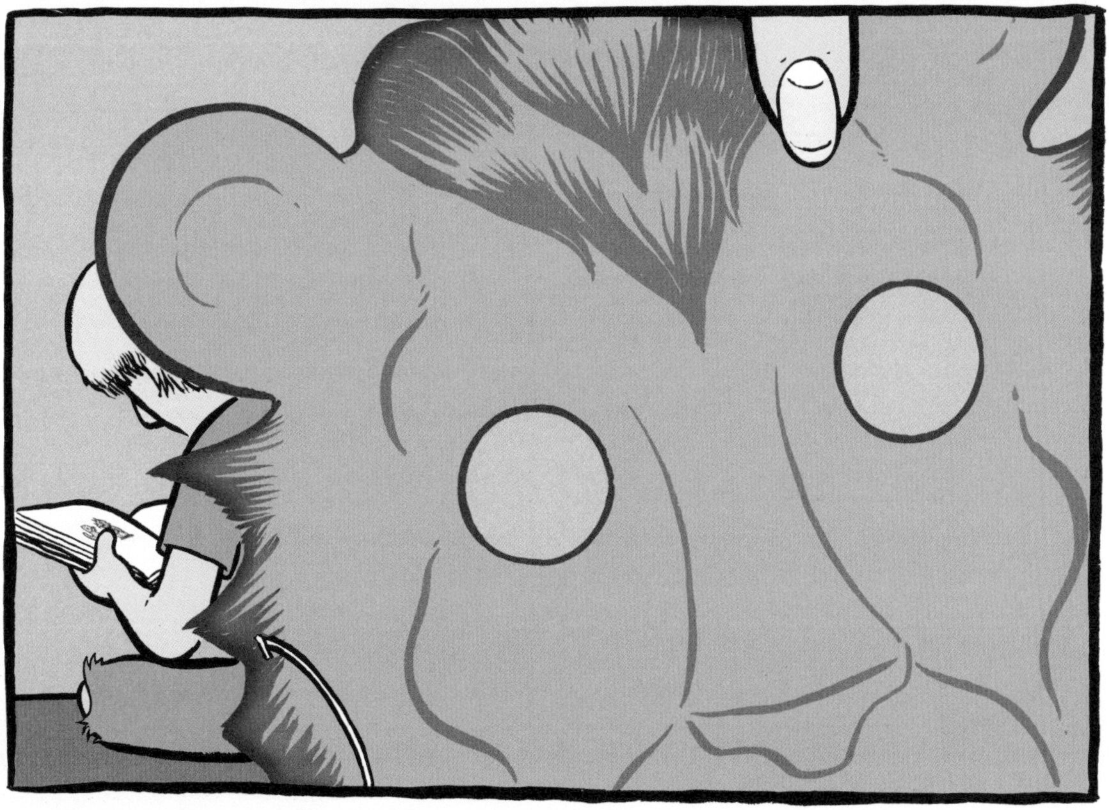

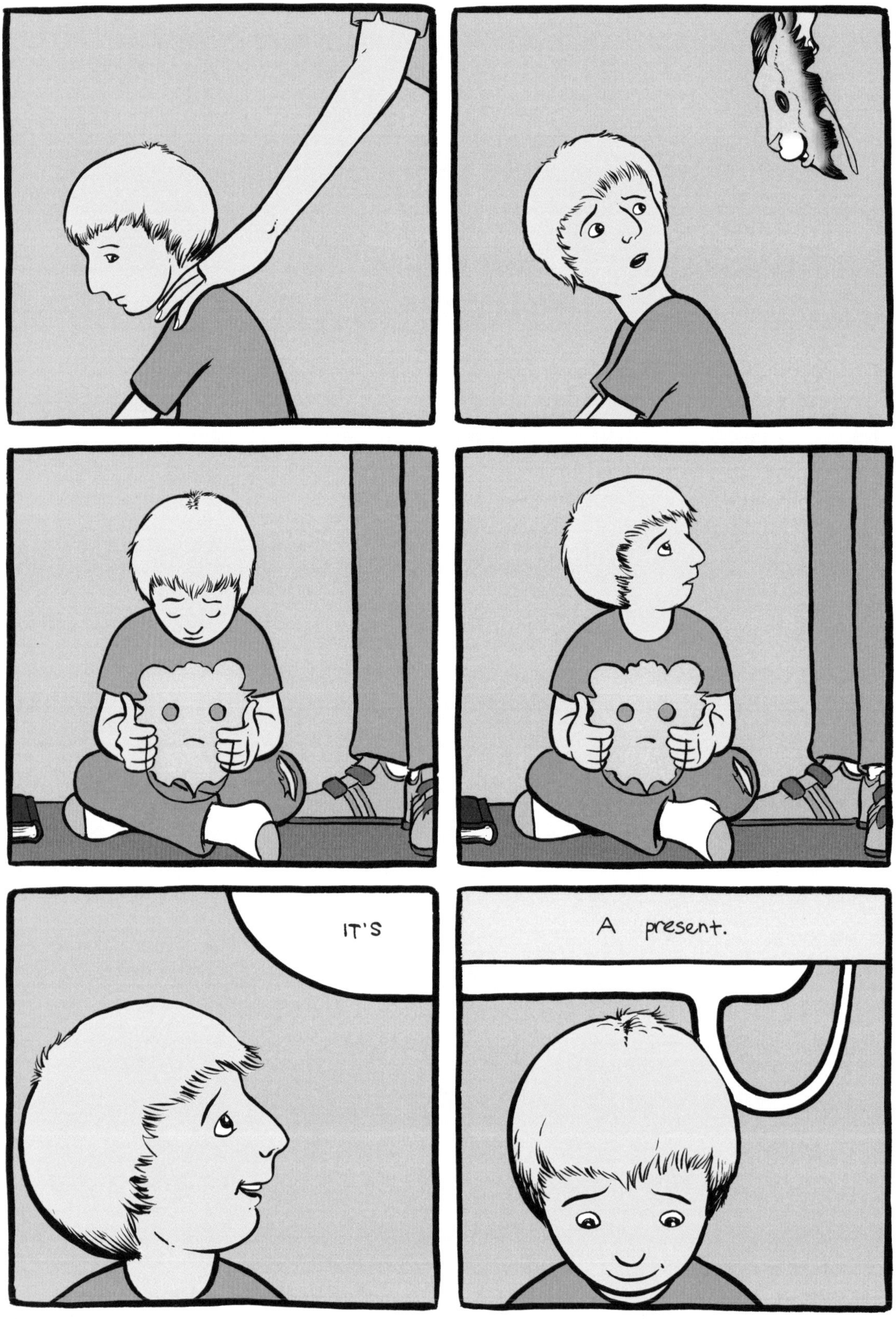
IT'S
A present.

That is one thing
I remember about my mother.

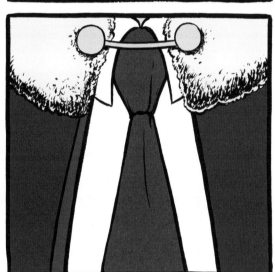

THANKS,
MOM.

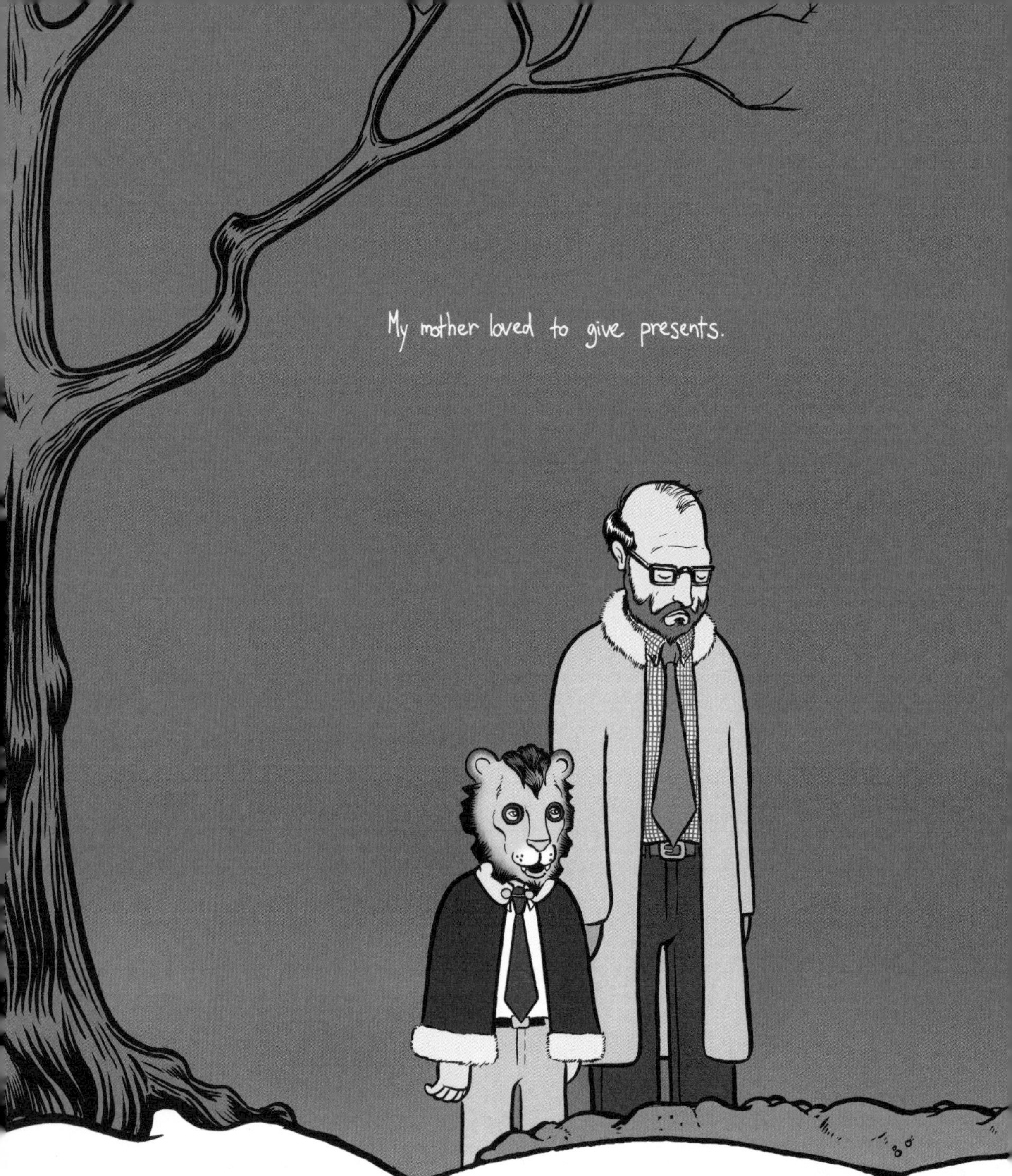
My mother loved to give presents.

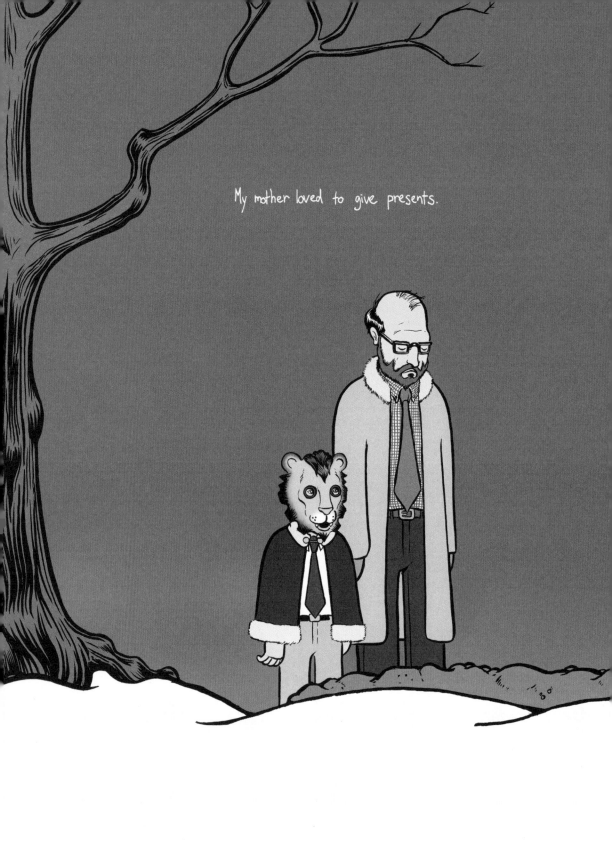

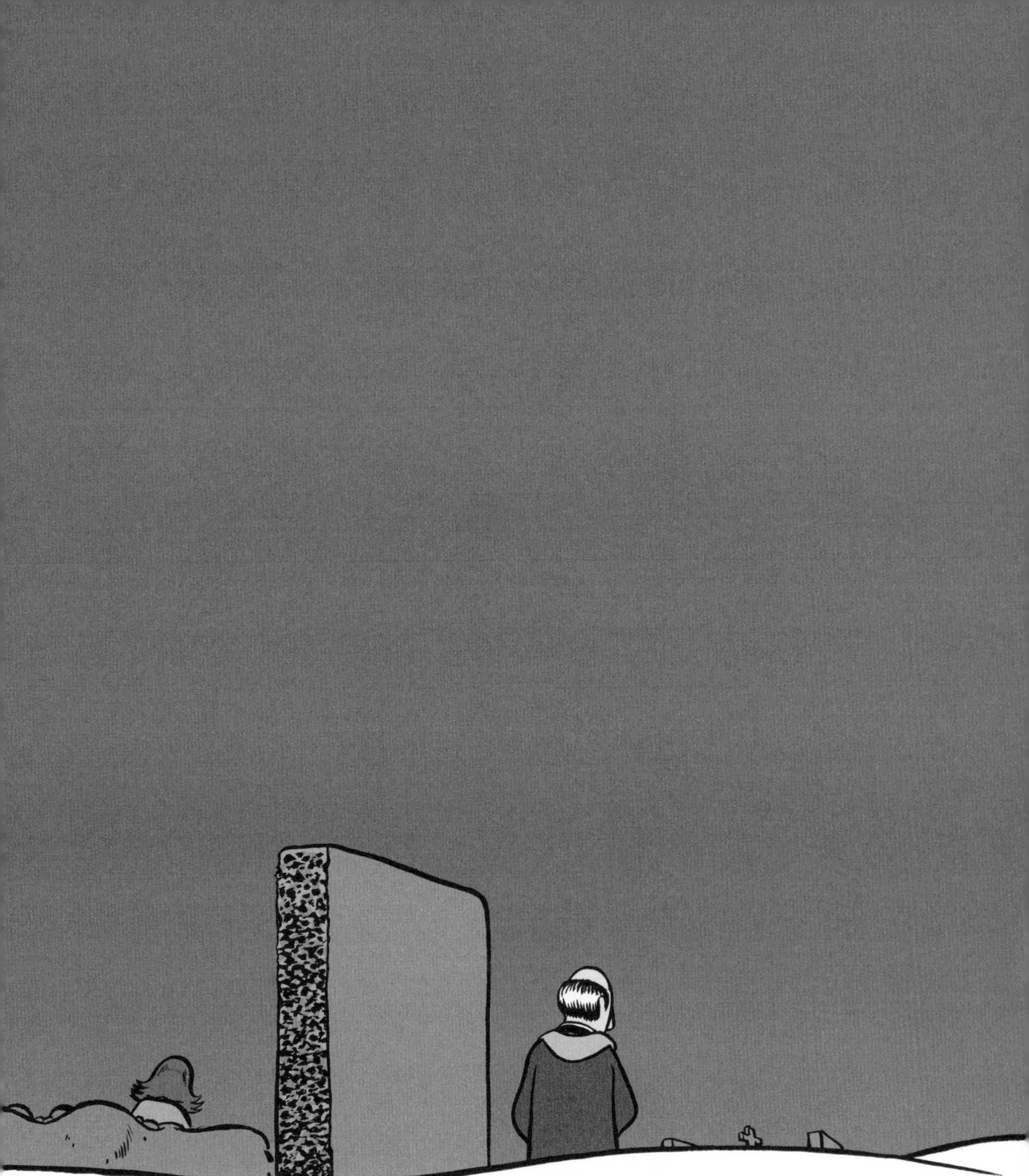

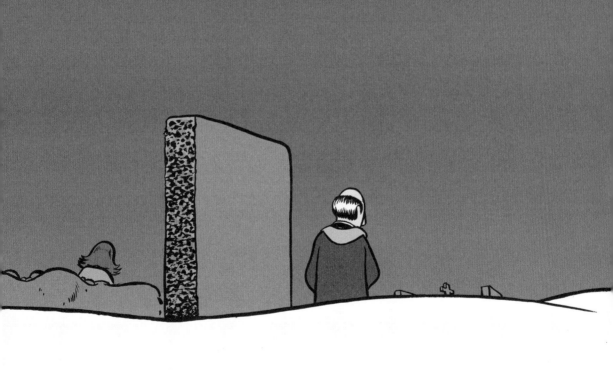

THOMAS?
HEY, COME ON
INSIDE! DINNER!

HOW'S
THE
FORT?

'S
OKAY.
I'LL
MAKE
IT BETTER
AFTER
DINNER.

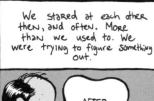

We stared at each other
then, and often. More
than we used to. We
were trying to figure something
out.

AFTER
DINNER?

YEAH.

Or trying very
hard NOT to.

LET'S...
UMM...

LET'S
SEE...

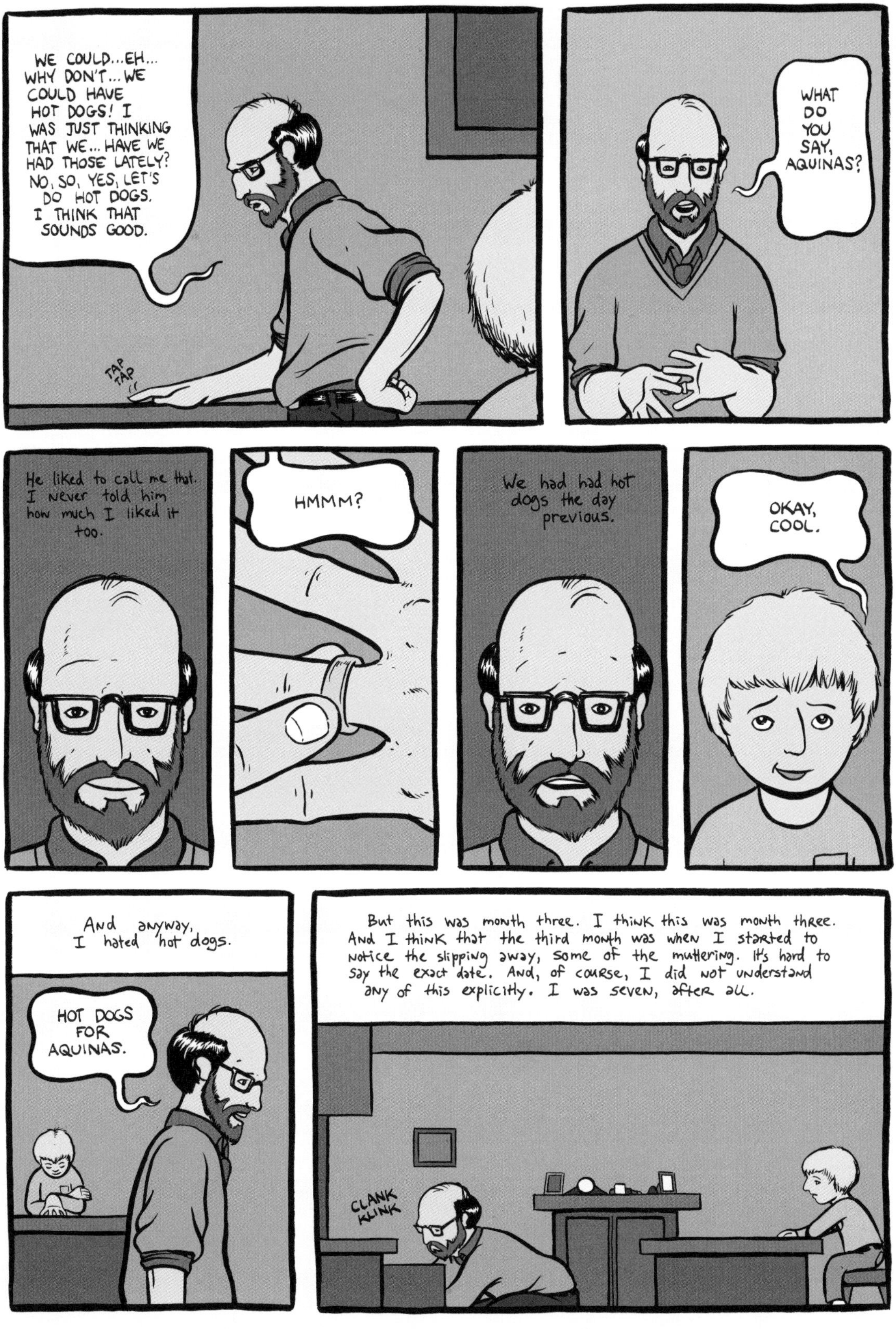

WE COULD...EH... WHY DON'T...WE COULD HAVE HOT DOGS! I WAS JUST THINKING THAT WE... HAVE WE HAD THOSE LATELY? NO, SO, YES, LET'S DO HOT DOGS. I THINK THAT SOUNDS GOOD.
TAP TAP
WHAT DO YOU SAY, AQUINAS?
He liked to call me that. I never told him how much I liked it too.
HMMM?
We had had hot dogs the day previous.
OKAY, COOL.
And anyway, I hated hot dogs.
HOT DOGS FOR AQUINAS.
But this was month three. I think this was month three. And I think that the third month was when I started to notice the slipping away, some of the muttering. It's hard to say the exact date. And, of course, I did not understand any of this explicitly. I was seven, after all.
CLANK KLINK

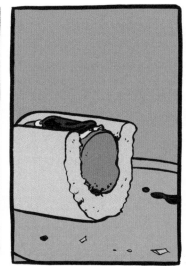

And I was busy with matters of my own.

KLINK

I was, in her absence, the groundskeeper, and these were my grounds:

Her garden, her room, her hiding place, the woods between.

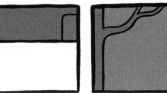

These were the areas over which I kept watch. These were significant areas, though the importance is muddled through a seven year-old's screen. Still, the sentiment common to all was all too clear: these were too powerfully **HERS**, and my father would not go near them.

So I kept them.

THE GARDEN

While it started as a group effort, the garden quickly became my mother's.

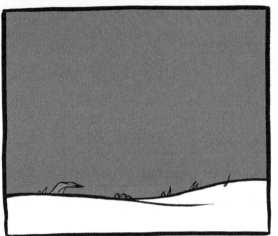

This sole proprietorship was strengthened after my father's second book, concerning the possibility of a broader application of symbolic logic, had unexpected mainstream (non-academia) success, causing a deep depression in him.

EVOLVING SYMBOLS

H.R. REEMELOUCI

He would sit and watch her weed the garden or watch her plant something brilliant.

He would grapple with the — at that time—possibility of the book edging him from associate to full professor.

She would assure him he was not "pandering to the ignorant."

He had just explained things perfectly, she would say, handing him a bruised lily.

THE ROOM

My father had moved out of the bedroom shortly after she left. Maybe a month. So I kept watch over it. I dusted it, I smacked at spiders.

The bed was moved to the attic space/ guest room, though he often did not sleep in it. A blanket was spread on the floor.

The floor of the attic space was thick with mildew, and worsened my father's allergies.

And, even worse, it was directly above my room.

I could hear him, mumbling through the boards.

Begging her.

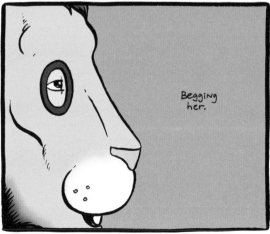

THE HIDING PLACE

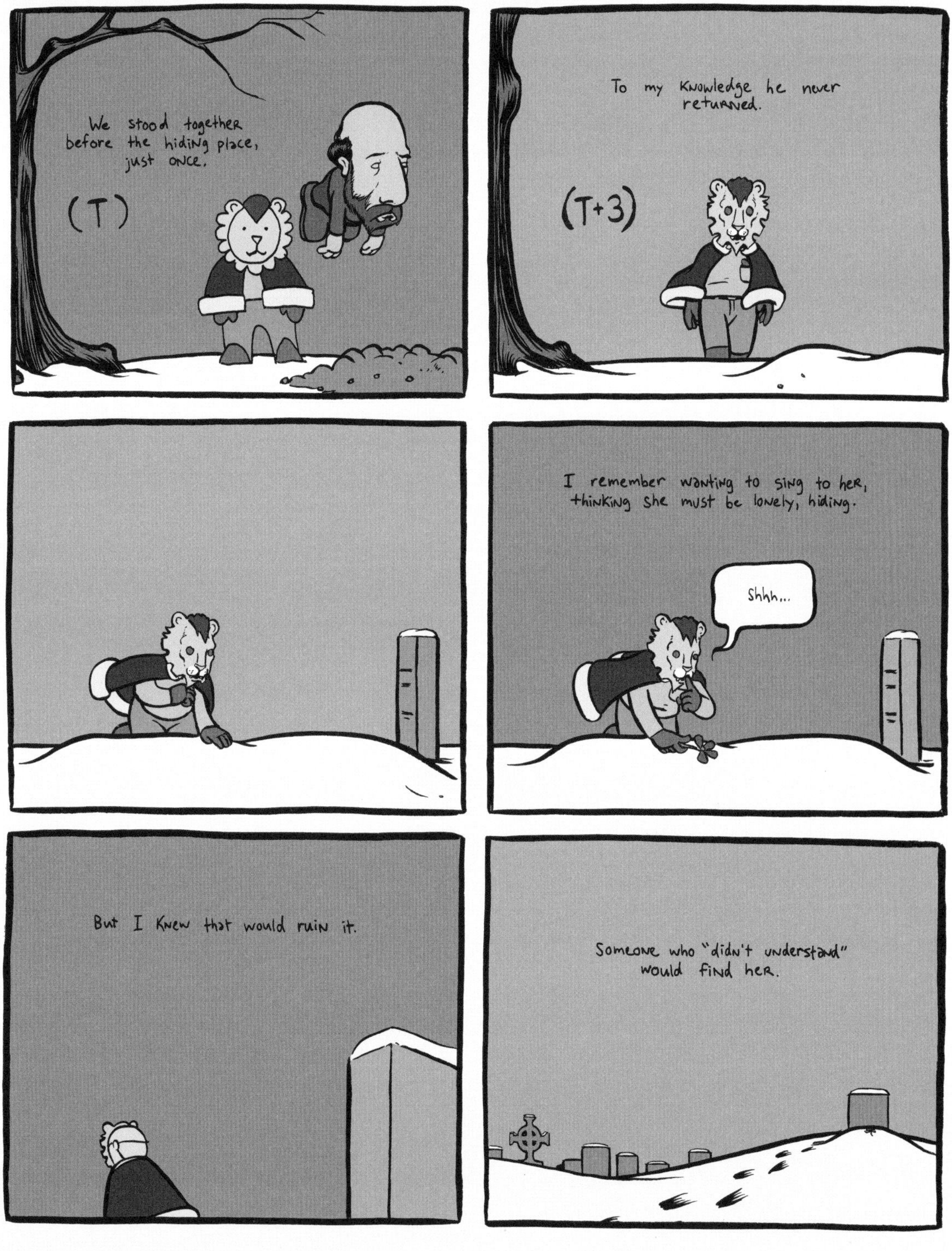

We stood together before the hiding place, just once.
(T)
To my knowledge he never returned.
(T+3)
I remember wanting to sing to her, thinking she must be lonely, hiding.
Shhh...
But I knew that would ruin it.
Someone who "didn't understand" would find her.

THE WOODS BETWEEN

This took me the longest to understand. My theory then was that these trees simply frightened my father (they frightened me). But, in looking through his journals again to write this edition's introduction, I found it.

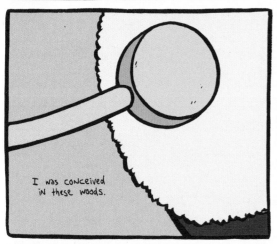

I was conceived in these woods.

My mother was the spontaneous counterpart to my father's logic, and she broke him one night in the leaves and sticks.

One night when they made me. One night when she needed his help.

Even now, woods hold something strange for me.

Again, it is difficult to recall when precisely I started to notice my father changing and completely erroneous to say I understood what the change meant or its extent, at least until the final point.

Little routines are the first victims of obsessive fantasy and escapism.

Little pieces from the previously regular wall of my father.

NAT'L IMAG

He would miss a performance or a game or some other public appearance function.

Dinner would not be served at 5:30 sharp (the way it had when he was a child, he would remind my mother and me).

A bill's payment would be sent later than seven days prior to its due date.

FIRST CLASS US POSTAGE PAID PRE-COMPANY

A graduate student, a teaching assistant named Steve, would call regarding my father missing a lecture. I would take a message and thank him for calling.

THANK YOU.

Taking messages from Steve and eventually more general scheduling were unavoidable realities.

KLACK

The groundskeeper needed to maintain a schedule...

And so I did, more and more...

... as my father sealed himself further into the recess, somewhere beneath my mother.

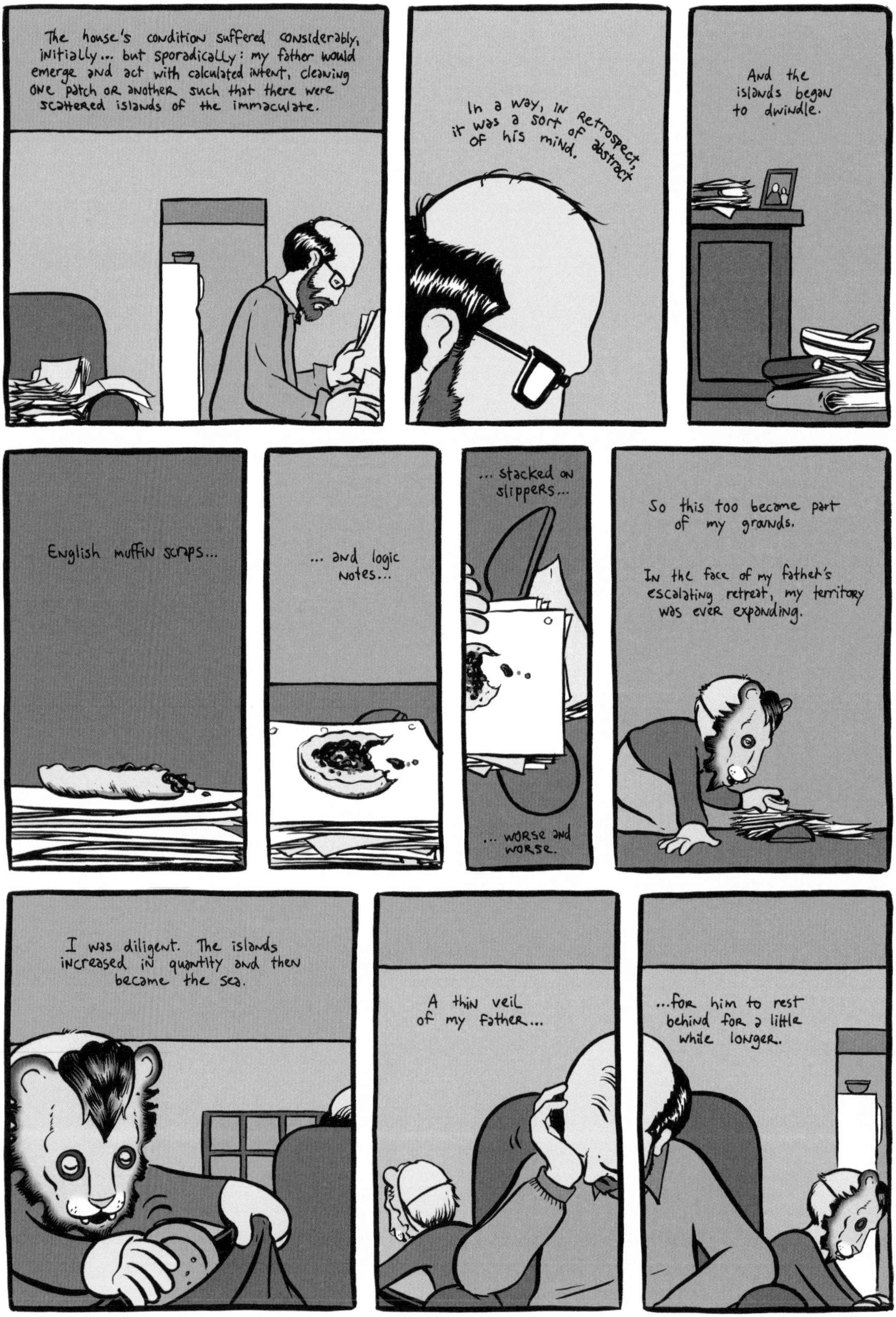
The house's condition suffered considerably, initially... but sporadically: my father would emerge and act with calculated intent, cleaning one patch or another such that there were scattered islands of the immaculate.
In a way, in retrospect, it was a sort of abstract of his mind.
And the islands began to dwindle.
English muffin scraps...
...and logic notes...
...stacked on slippers...
...worse and worse.
So this too became part of my grounds.
In the face of my father's escalating retreat, my territory was ever expanding.
I was diligent. The islands increased in quantity and then became the sea.
A thin veil of my father...
...for him to rest behind for a little while longer.

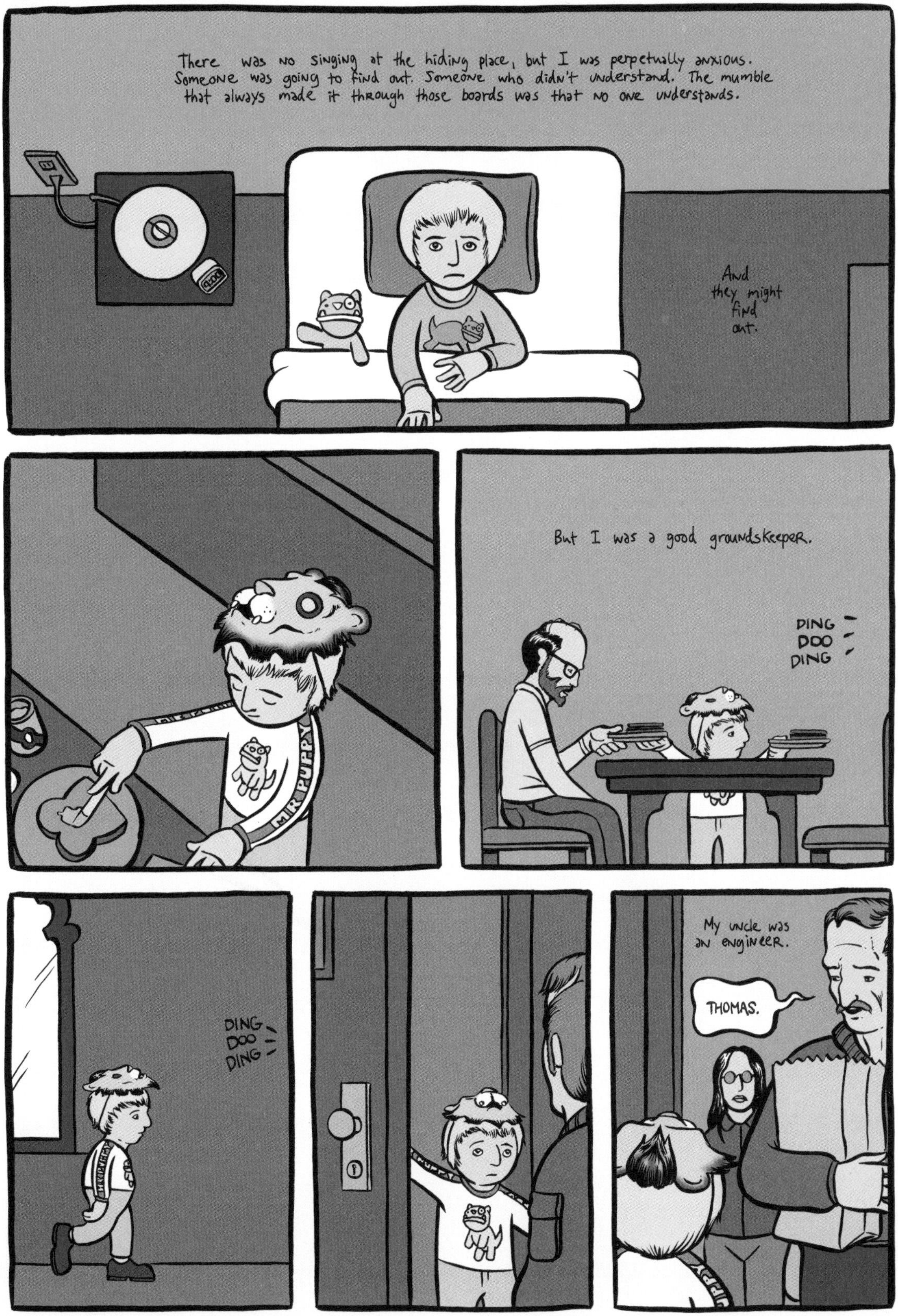
There was no singing at the hiding place, but I was perpetually anxious. Someone was going to find out. Someone who didn't understand. The mumble that always made it through those boards was that no one understands.
And they might find out.
MR PUPPY
But I was a good groundskeeper.
DING DOO DING
DING DOO DING
My uncle was an engineer.
THOMAS.

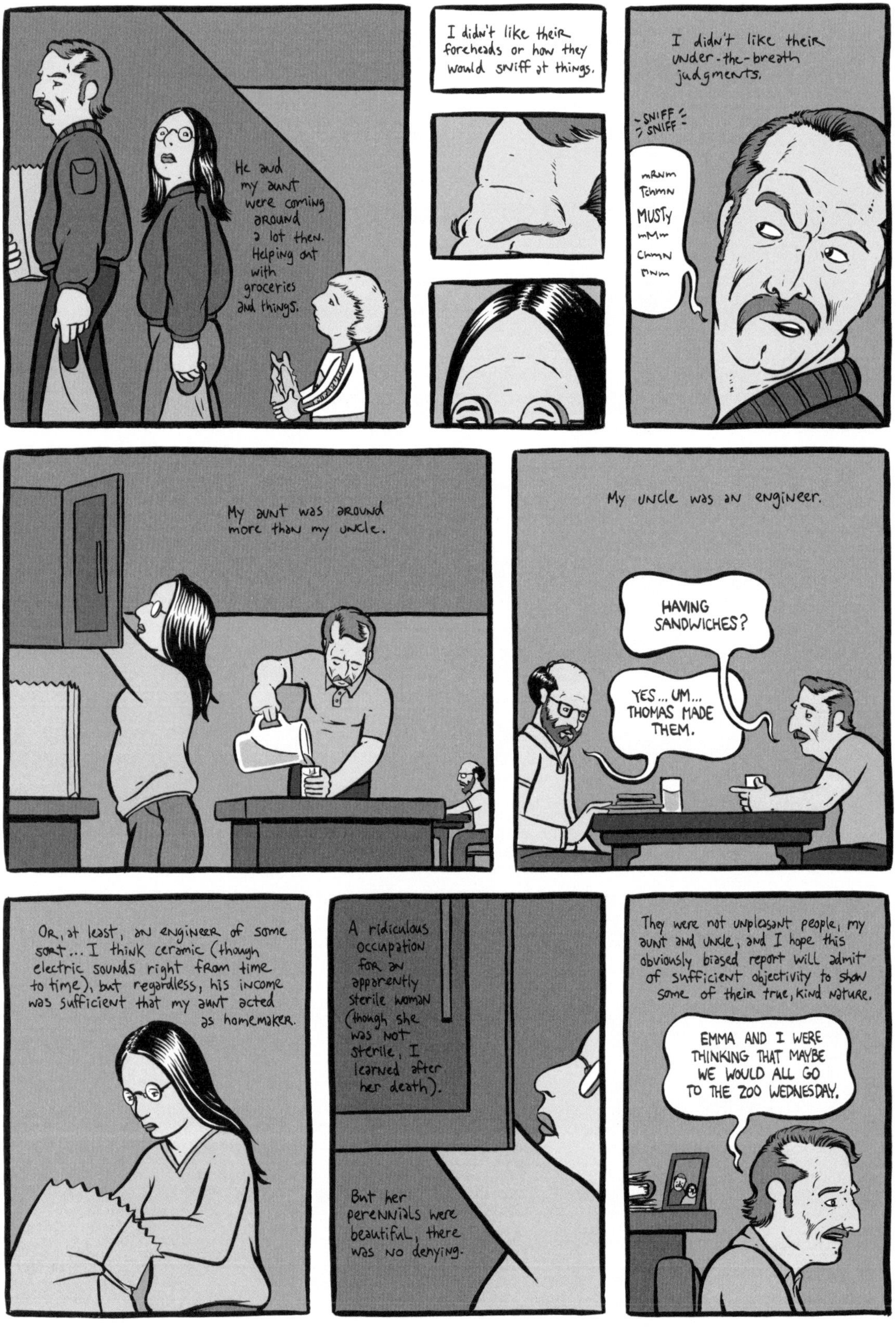
He and my aunt were coming around a lot then. Helping out with groceries and things.
I didn't like their foreheads or how they would sniff at things.
I didn't like their under-the-breath judgments.
SNIFF SNIFF
mRNm Tchmn MUSTy mMm ChmN mNm
My aunt was around more than my uncle.
My uncle was an engineer.
HAVING SANDWICHES?
YES... UM... THOMAS MADE THEM.
Or, at least, an engineer of some sort... I think ceramic (though electric sounds right from time to time), but regardless, his income was sufficient that my aunt acted as homemaker.
A ridiculous occupation for an apparently sterile woman (though she was not sterile, I learned after her death).
But her perennials were beautiful, there was no denying.
They were not unpleasant people, my aunt and uncle, and I hope this obviously biased report will admit of sufficient objectivity to show some of their true, kind nature.
EMMA AND I WERE THINKING THAT MAYBE WE WOULD ALL GO TO THE ZOO WEDNESDAY.

Days and rote months passed without incident.

Without singing.

Everything tried

So hard

that spring.

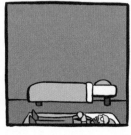

We can't be blamed for lack of effort.

READY?

YEAH.

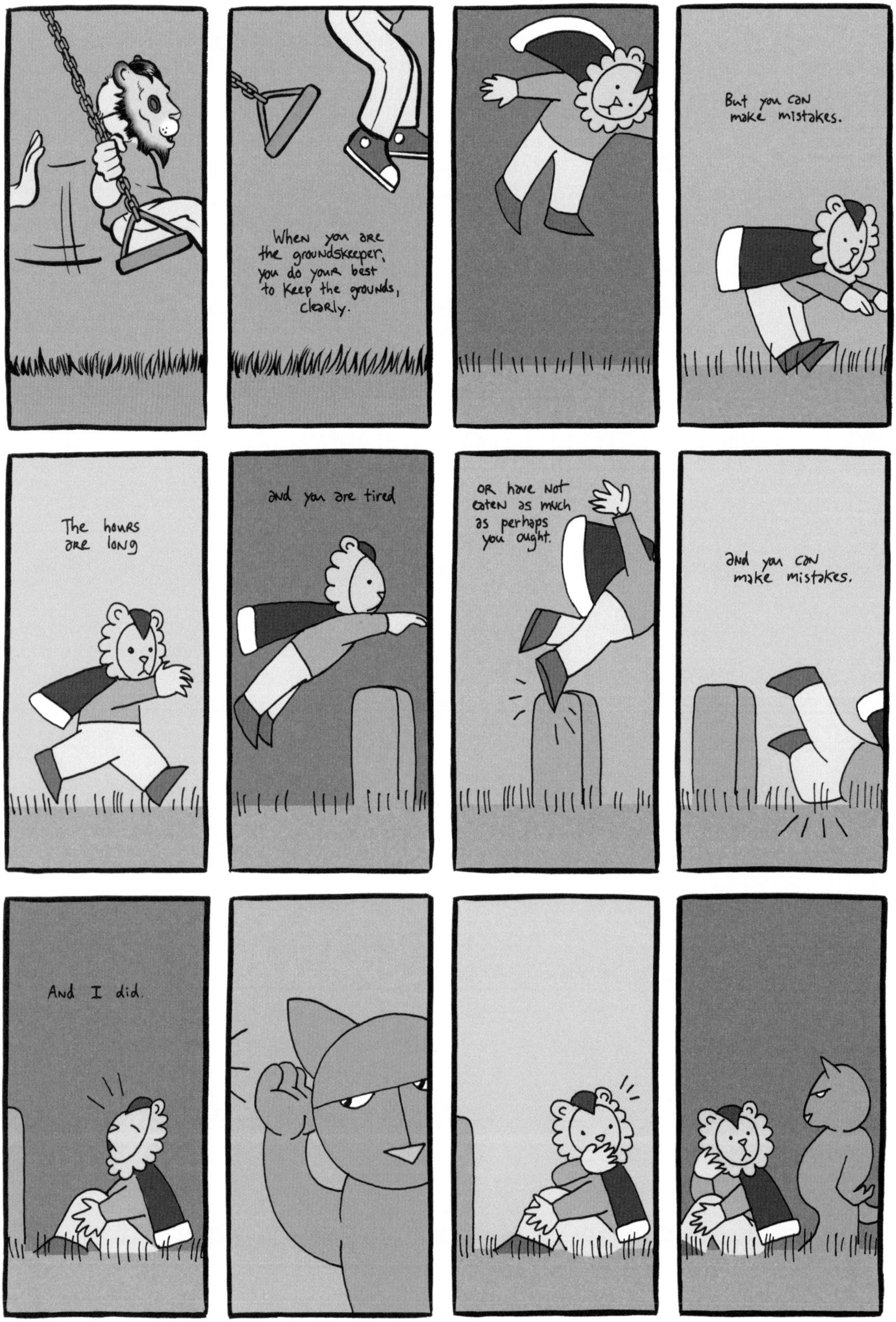
When you are the groundskeeper, you do your best to keep the grounds, clearly.
But you can make mistakes.
The hours are long
and you are tired
or have not eaten as much as perhaps you ought.
and you can make mistakes.
And I did.

This was my mistake:

HELLO?
THIS IS THE
TENNANTS'?

HELLO.

OH! HANG ON, STEVE,
THE PEN'S ON THE
COUNTER... JUST A
MINUTE.

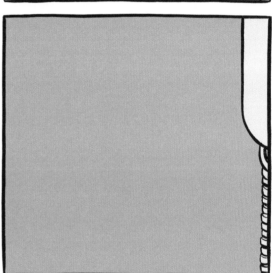

OKAY... GO AHEAD.

WITH
WHAT?

WITH WHAT I SHOULD TELL MY DAD. ABOUT WHATEVER LECTURE HE MISSED.
HE MISSED A LECTURE?
WELL... YEAH, JUST LIKE LAST...
WAIT, DIDN'T HE?
HAS HE BEEN MISSING A LOT OF LECTURES THEN?
May... May I ask who's calling?
THIS IS YOUR UNCLE EDMUND, THOMAS.

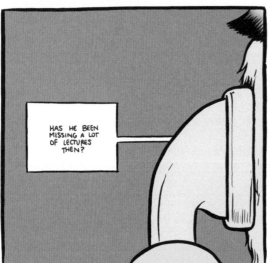

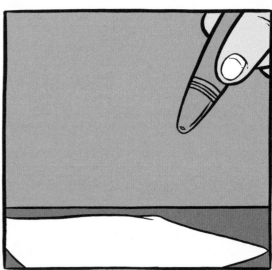

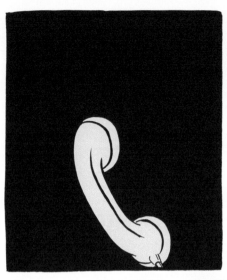

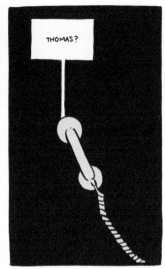
THOMAS?

THOMAS?

Y... YES?

IS YOUR FATHER THERE?

WELL... HE'S... YEAH, HE'S IN HIS ROOM, BUT...

WE'LL BE OVER SOON. MAYBE YOUR AUNT WILL MAKE US SOME OF HER SPAGHETTI.

I was hungry and tired.

And now they knew.

They were not unpleasant people, my aunt and uncle, and I hope that this obviously biased report will admit of sufficient objectivity to show some of their true, kind nature.

In my later twenties, I actually became good friends with my uncle, who was an understanding and forgiving man.

We needed each other in an odd way, he having lost his wife when I was twenty-one to the same cancer that took his sister, my mother.

I also think he missed my father, with whom he used to golf and of whom he was always respectfully envious for having successfully conceived a child.

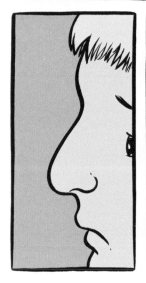

This was

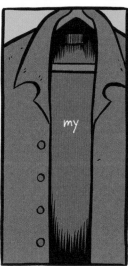

my

mistake.

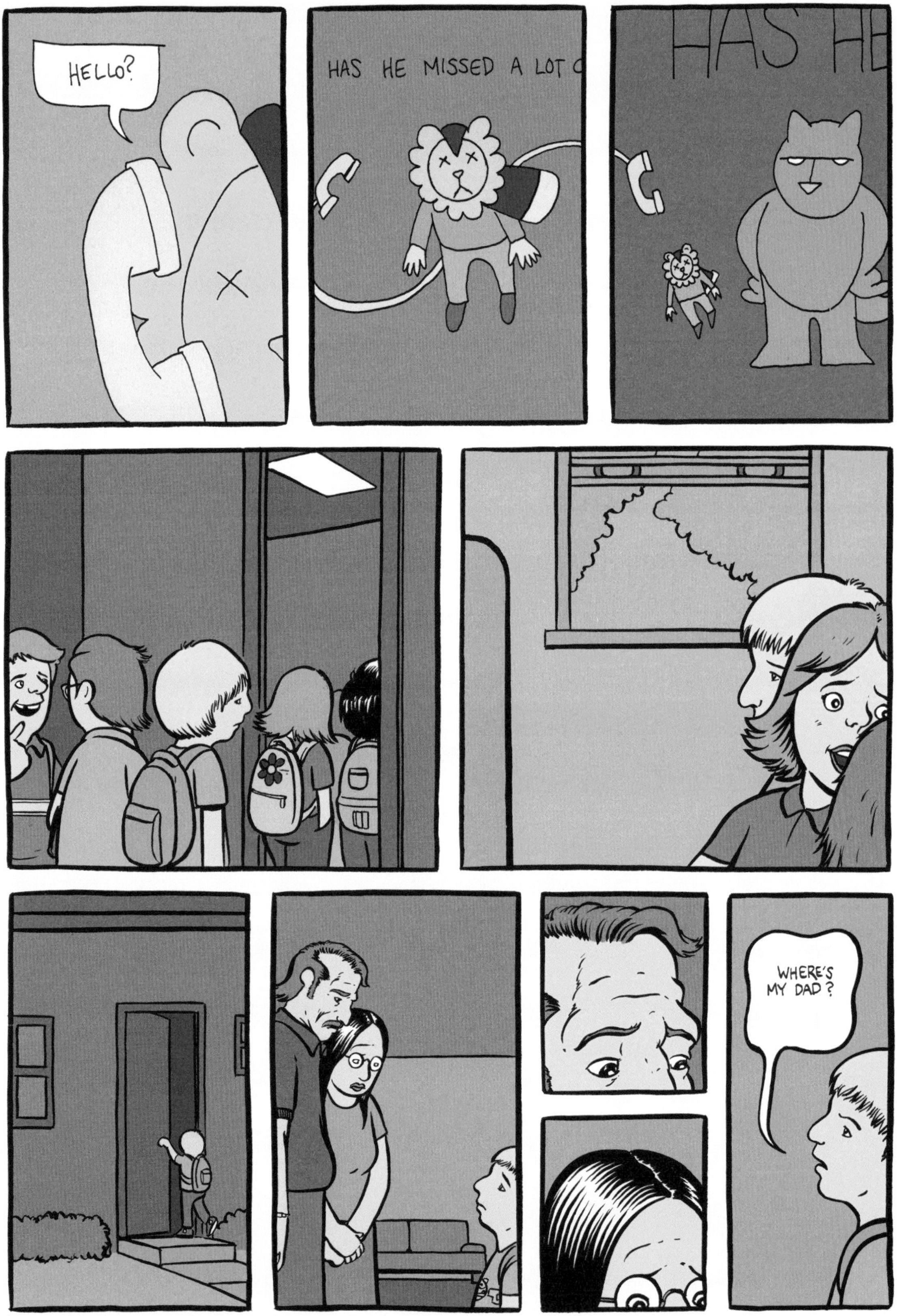
HELLO?
HAS HE MISSED A LOT
HAS HE
WHERE'S MY DAD?

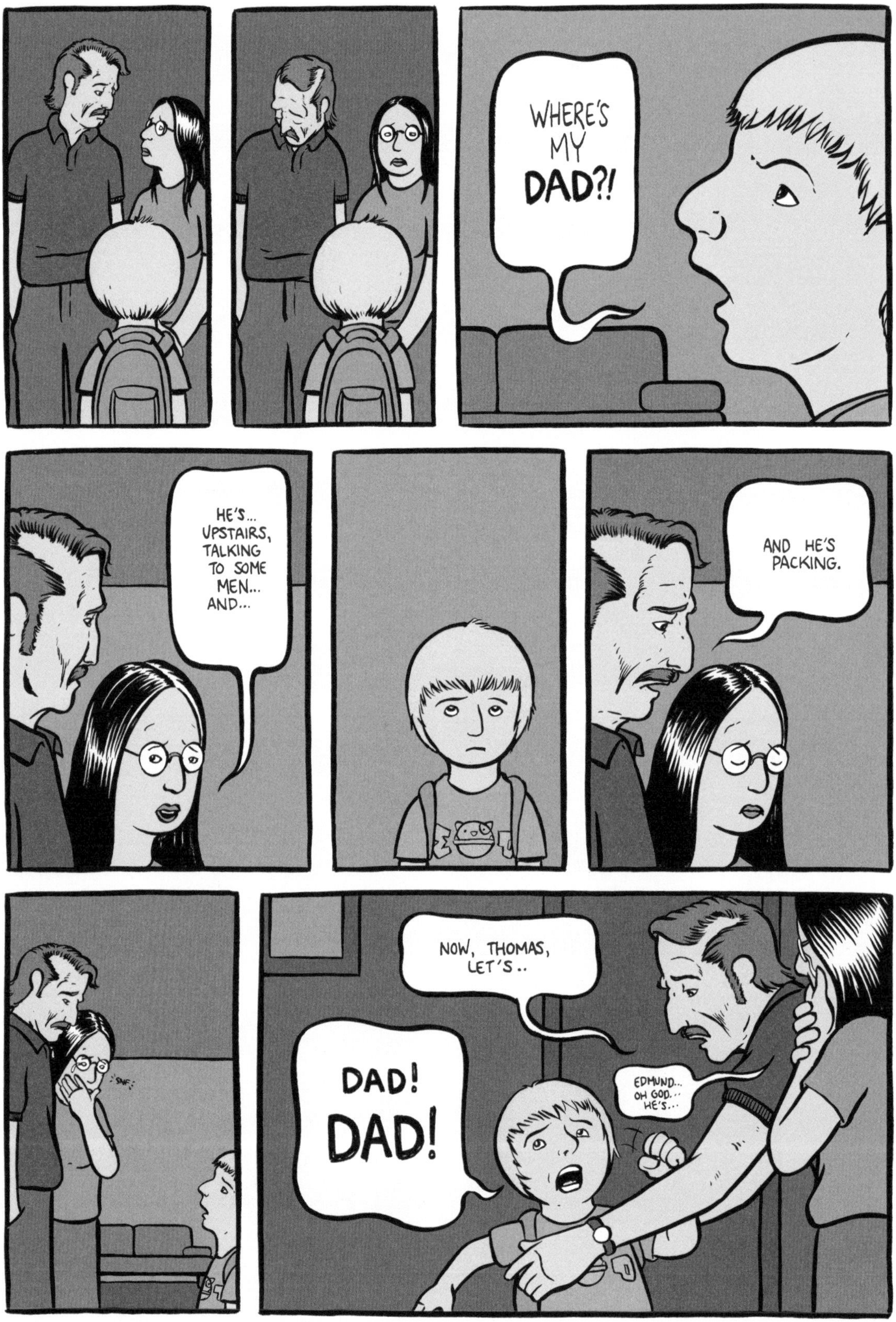
WHERE'S MY DAD?!
HE'S... UPSTAIRS, TALKING TO SOME MEN... AND...
AND HE'S PACKING.
SNF
NOW, THOMAS, LET'S..
DAD! DAD!
EDMUND... OH GOD... HE'S...

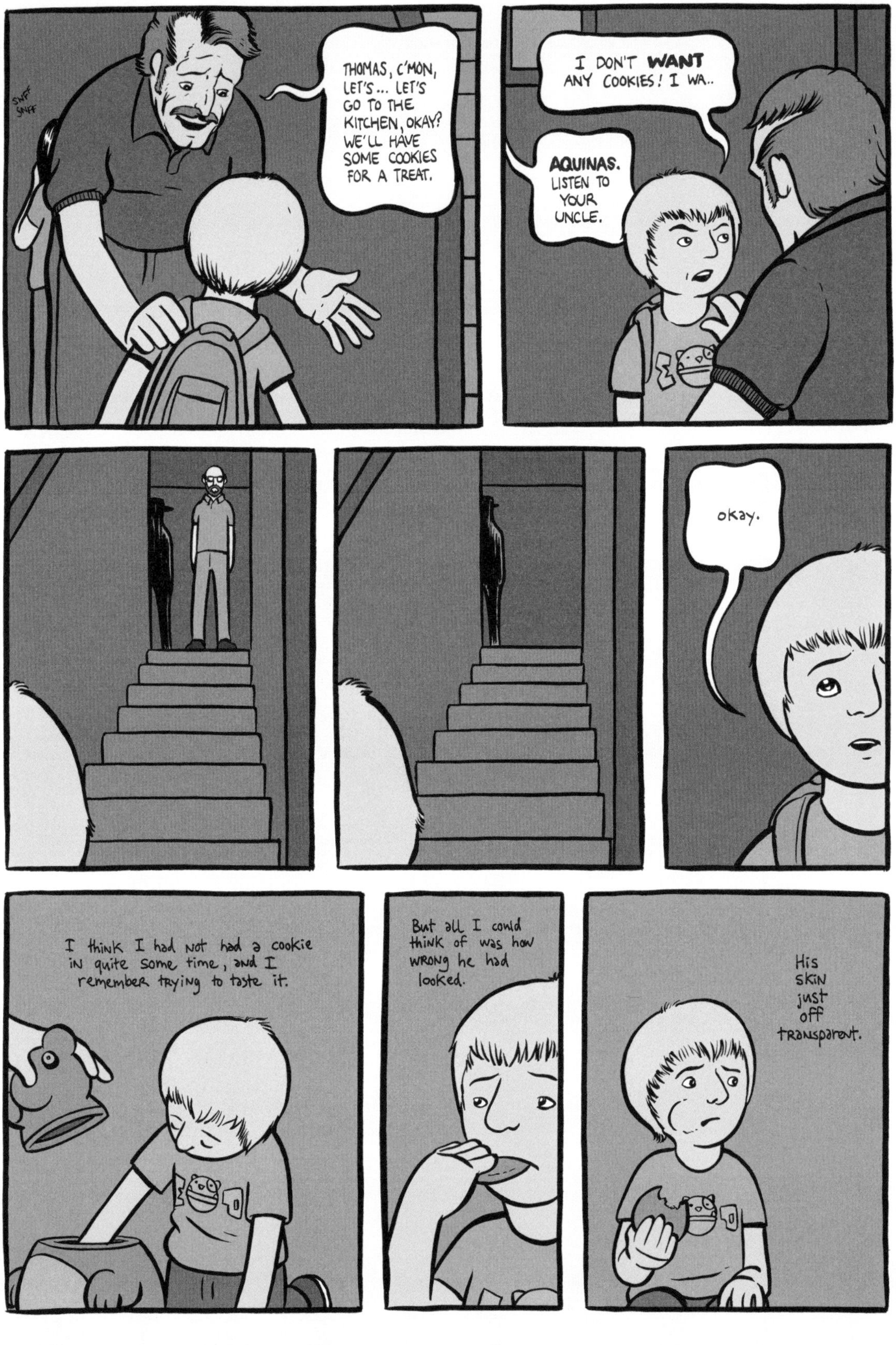
SNFF SNFF
THOMAS, C'MON, LET'S... LET'S GO TO THE KITCHEN, OKAY? WE'LL HAVE SOME COOKIES FOR A TREAT.
I DON'T **WANT** ANY COOKIES! I WA..
AQUINAS. LISTEN TO YOUR UNCLE.
okay.
I think I had not had a cookie in quite some time, and I remember trying to taste it.
But all I could think of was how WRONG he had looked.
His SKIN just off transparent.

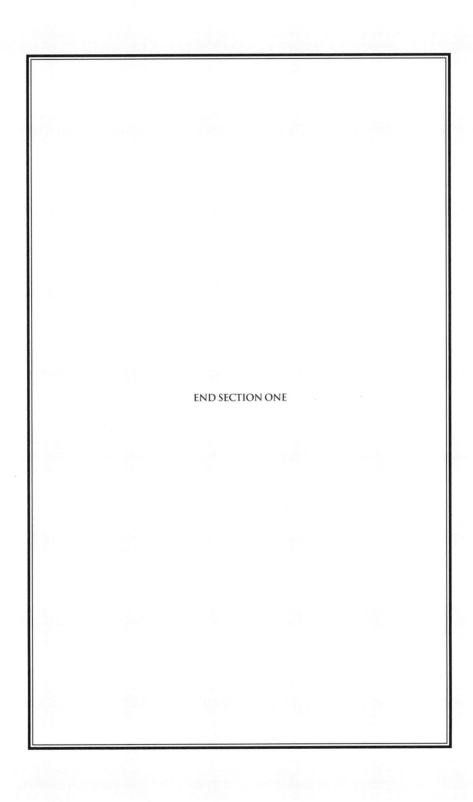

END SECTION ONE

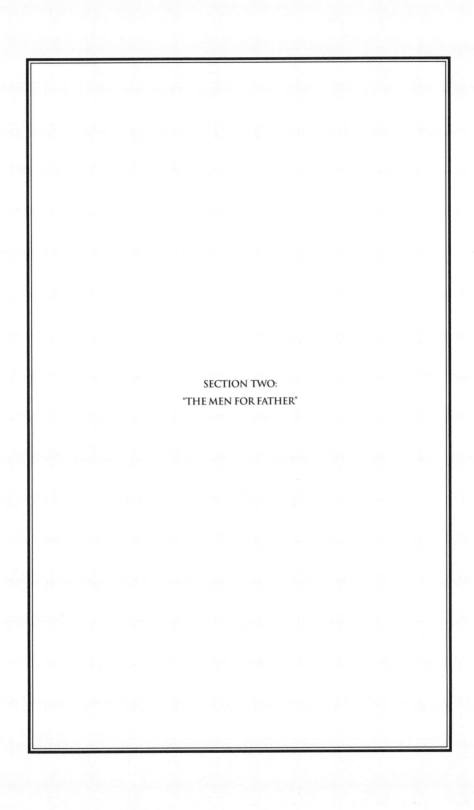

SECTION TWO:
"THE MEN FOR FATHER"

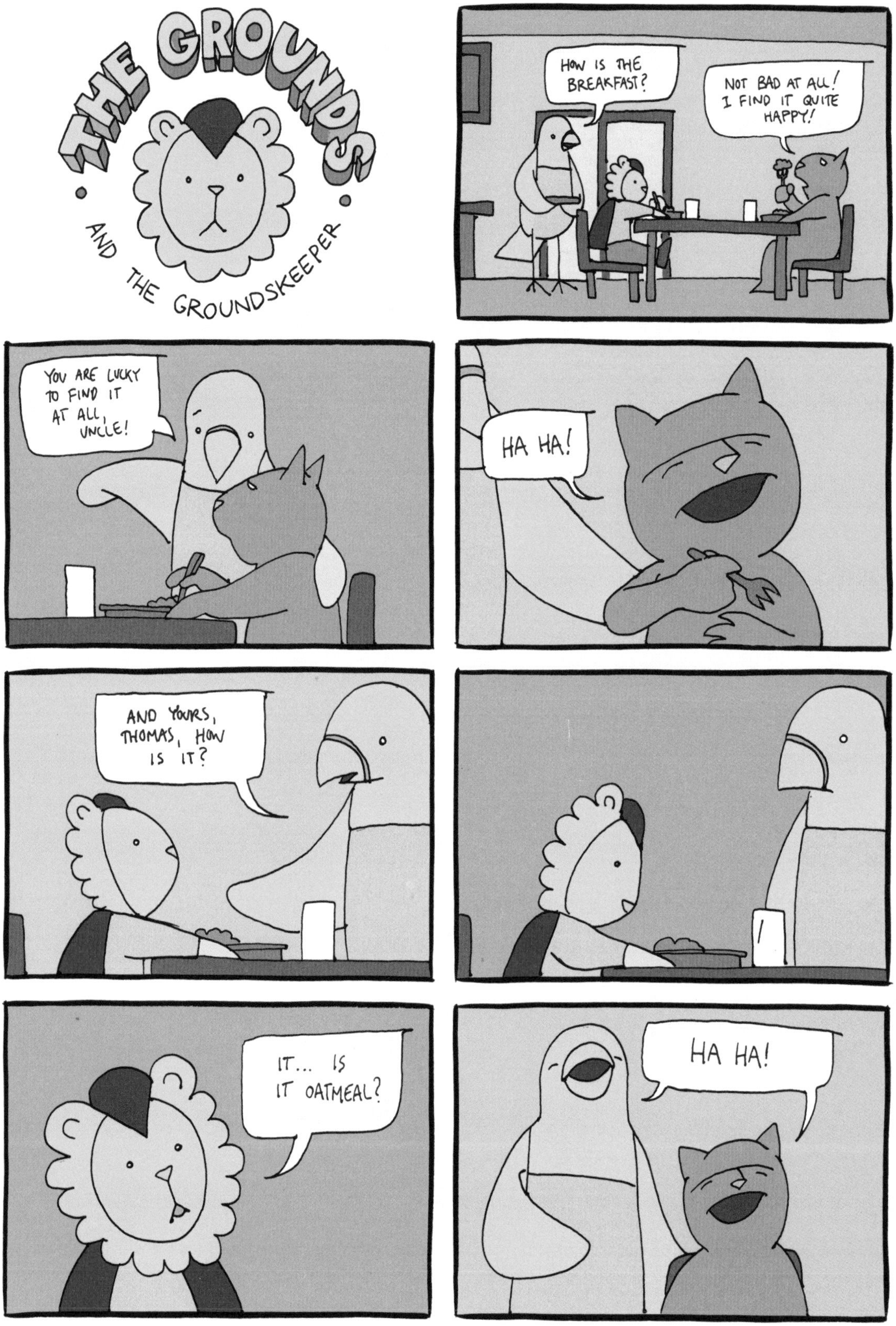
THE GROUNDS
AND THE GROUNDSKEEPER
HOW IS THE BREAKFAST?
NOT BAD AT ALL! I FIND IT QUITE HAPPY!
YOU ARE LUCKY TO FIND IT AT ALL, UNCLE!
HA HA!
AND YOURS, THOMAS, HOW IS IT?
IT... IS IT OATMEAL?
HA HA!

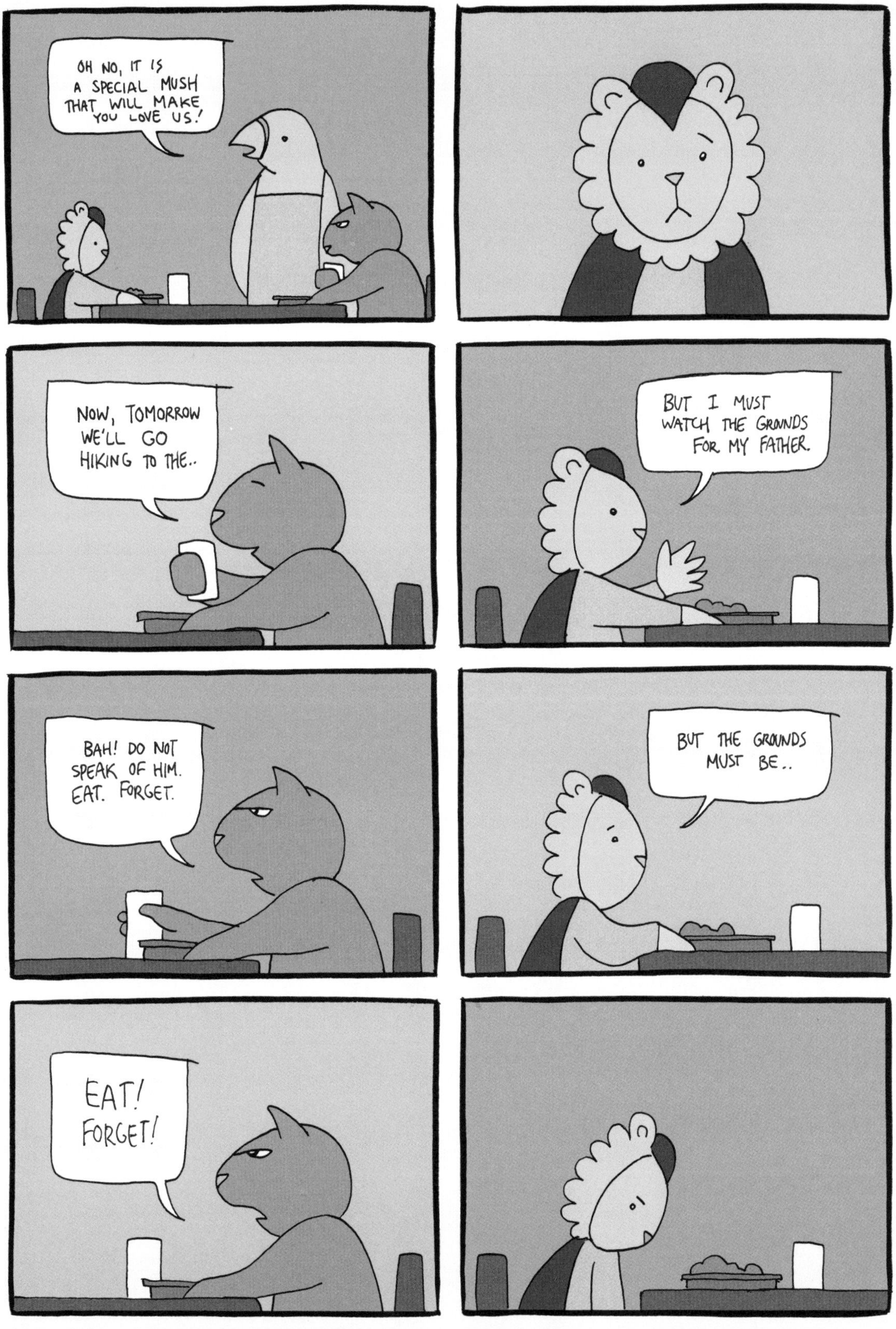
OH NO, IT IS A SPECIAL MUSH THAT WILL MAKE YOU LOVE US!
NOW, TOMORROW WE'LL GO HIKING TO THE..
BUT I MUST WATCH THE GROUNDS FOR MY FATHER.
BAH! DO NOT SPEAK OF HIM. EAT. FORGET.
BUT THE GROUNDS MUST BE..
EAT! FORGET!

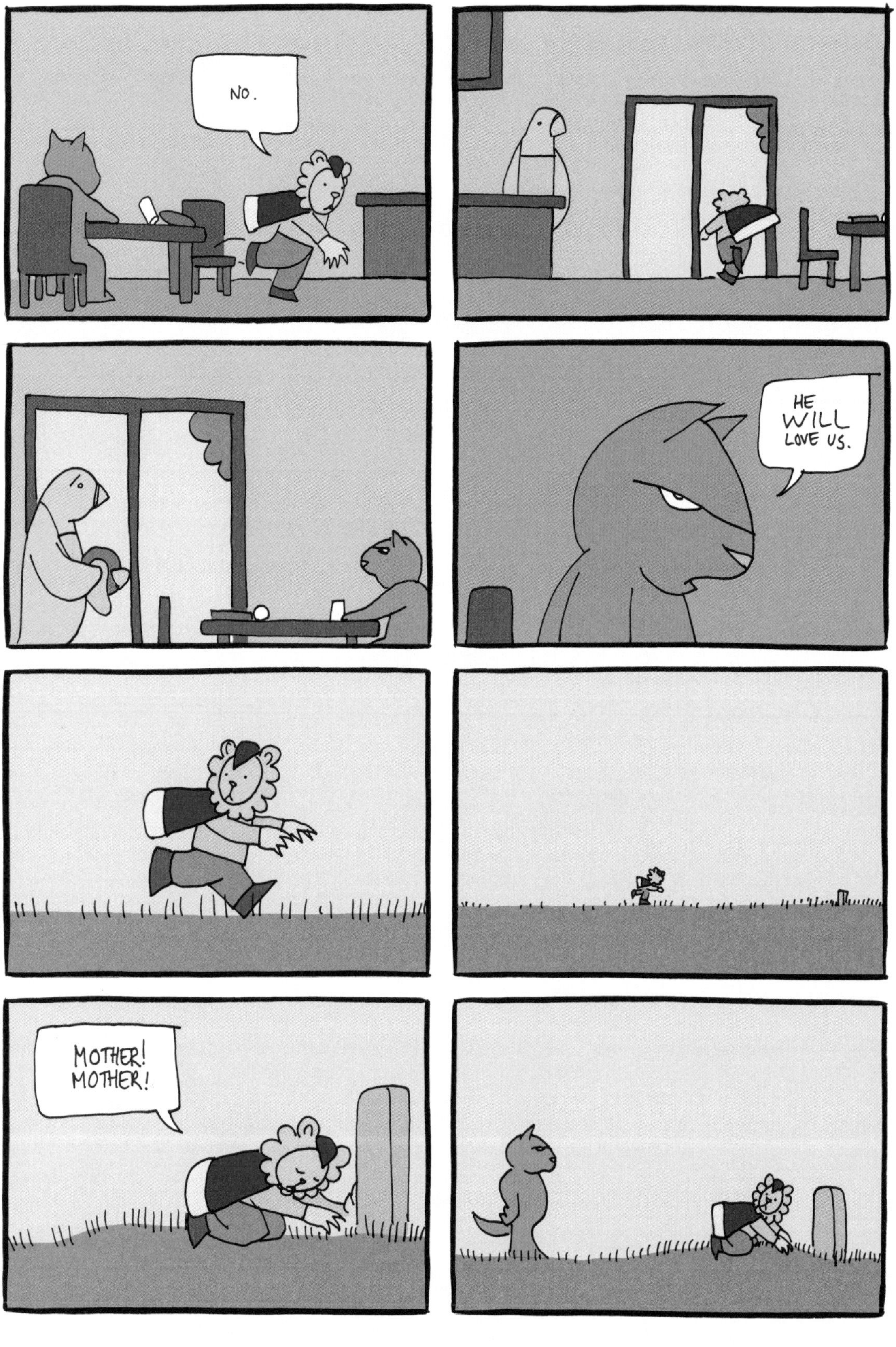
NO.
HE WILL LOVE US.
MOTHER! MOTHER!

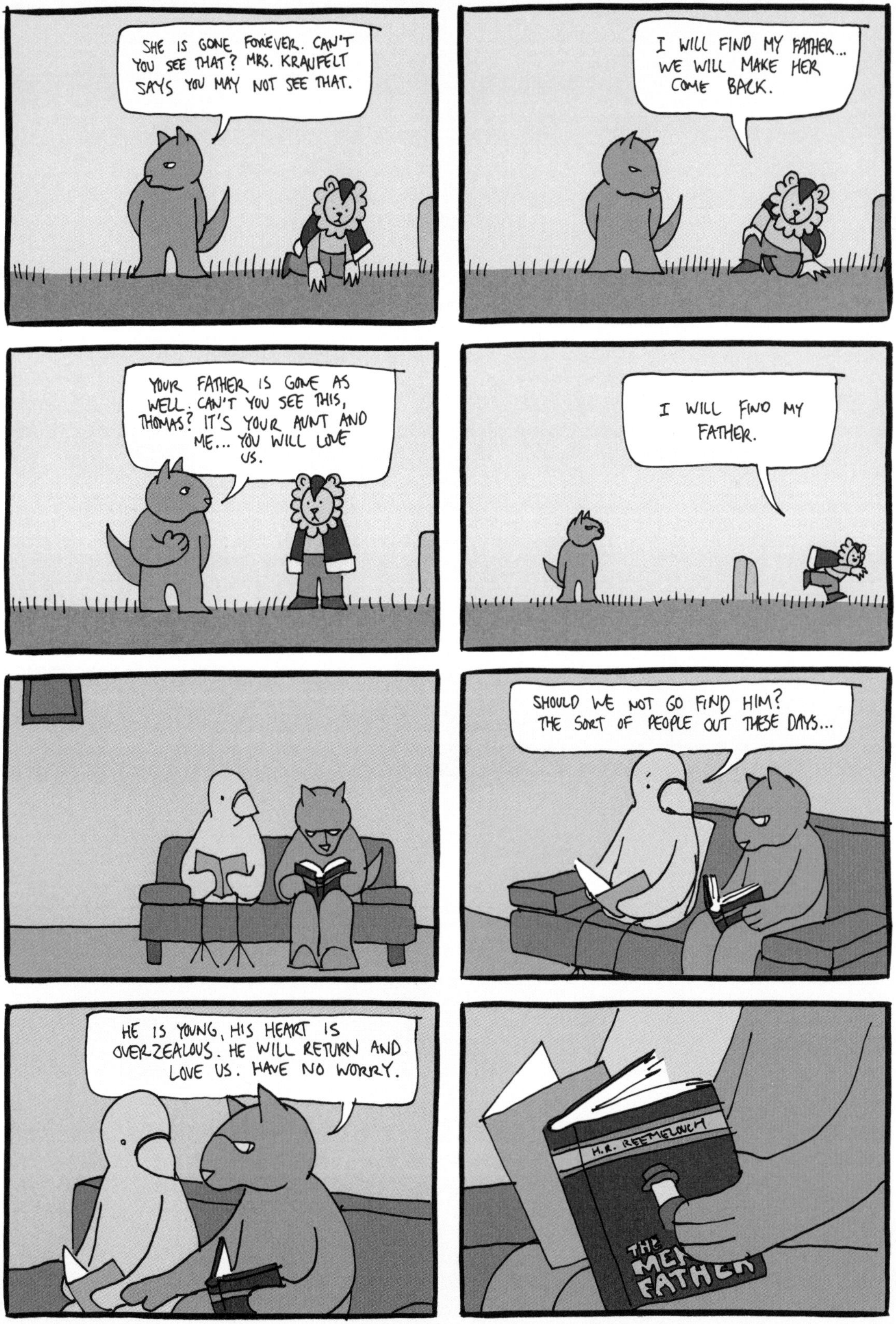

SHE IS GONE FOREVER. CAN'T YOU SEE THAT? MRS. KRAUFELT SAYS YOU MAY NOT SEE THAT.
I WILL FIND MY FATHER... WE WILL MAKE HER COME BACK.
YOUR FATHER IS GONE AS WELL. CAN'T YOU SEE THIS, THOMAS? IT'S YOUR AUNT AND ME... YOU WILL LOVE US.
I WILL FIND MY FATHER.
SHOULD WE NOT GO FIND HIM? THE SORT OF PEOPLE OUT THESE DAYS...
HE IS YOUNG, HIS HEART IS OVERZEALOUS. HE WILL RETURN AND LOVE US. HAVE NO WORRY.
H.R. REEMELOUCH
THE ME
FATHER

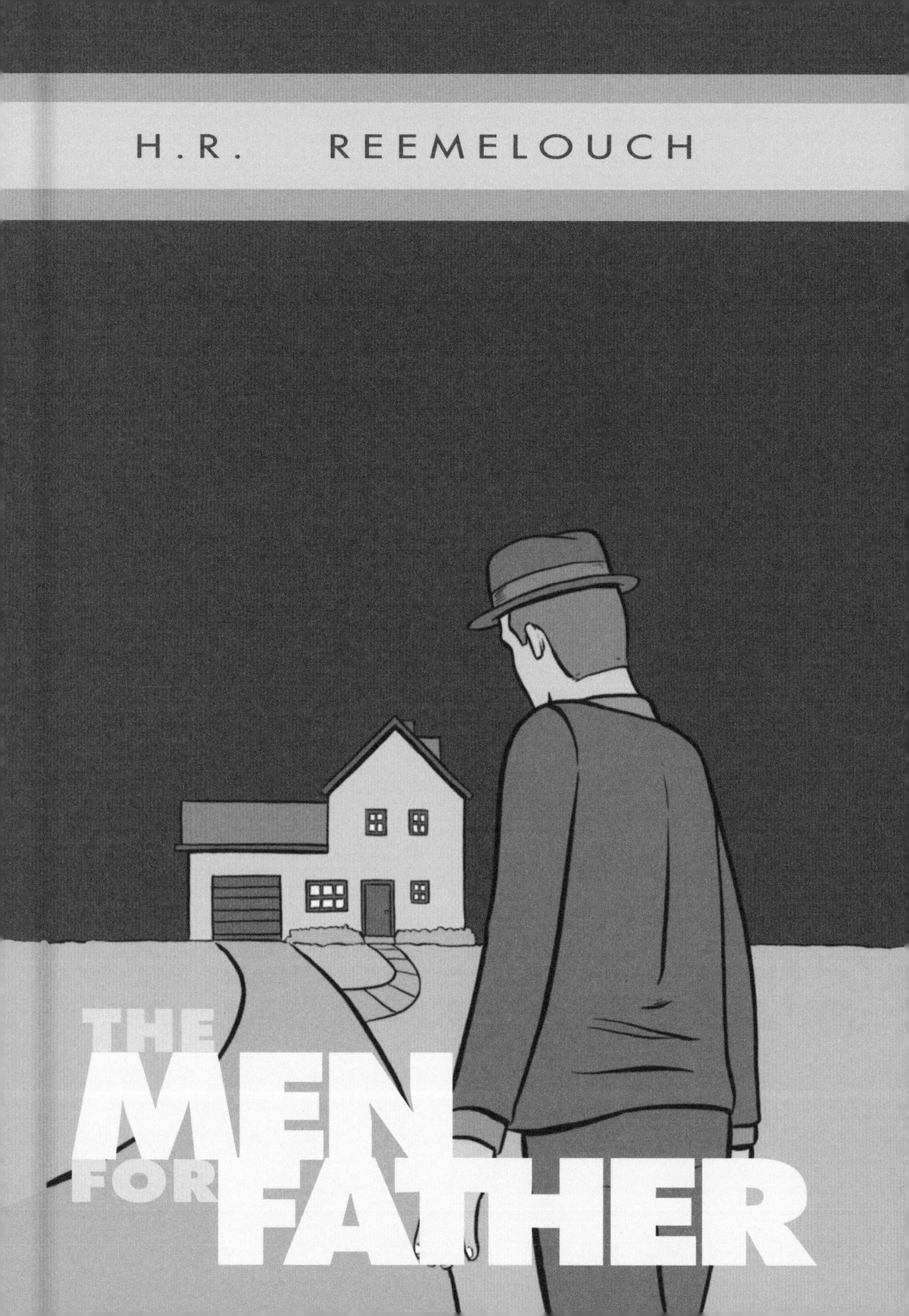
H.R. REEMELOUCH
THE MEN FOR FATHER

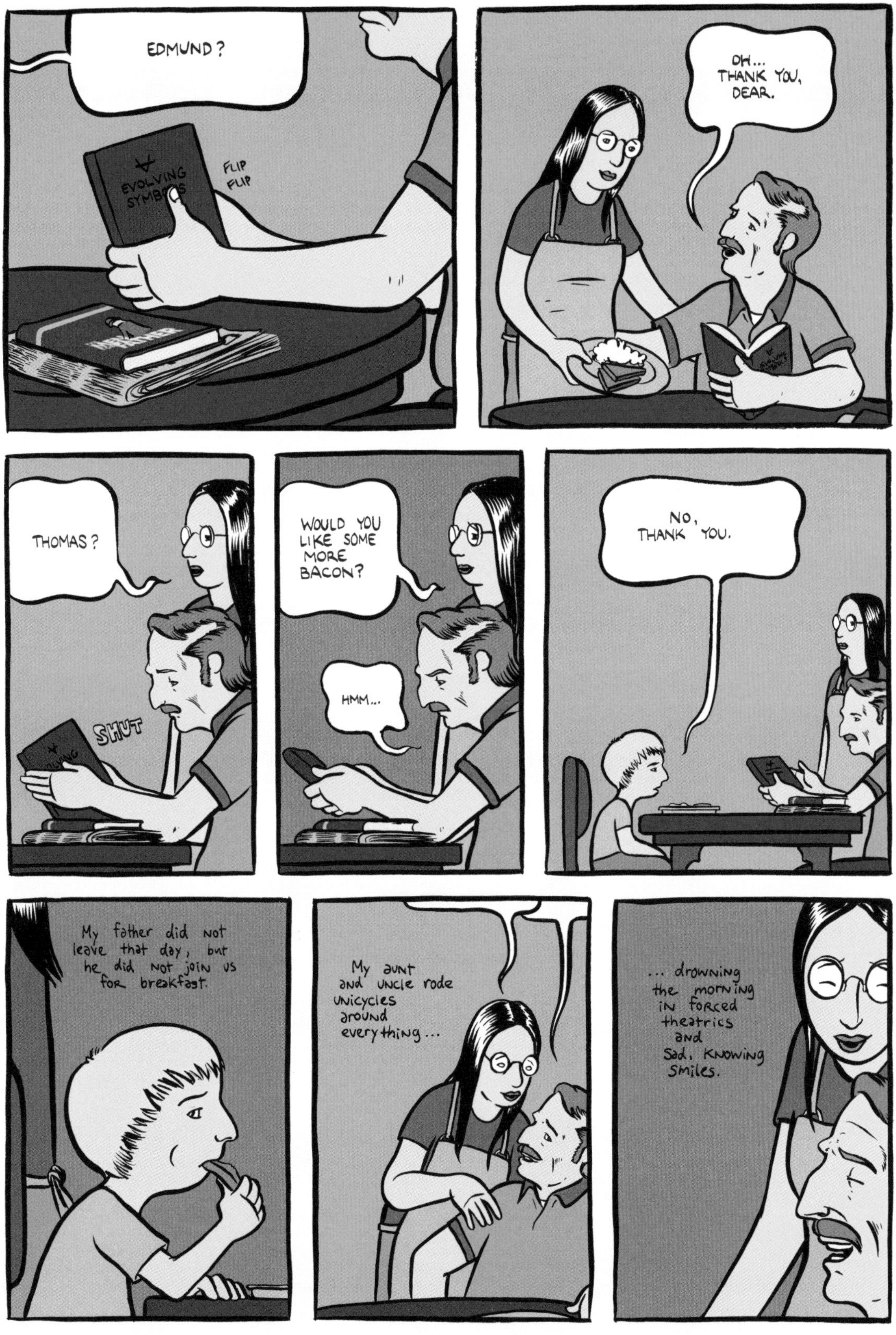
EDMUND?
EVOLVING SYMBOLS
FLIP FLIP
OH... THANK YOU, DEAR.
THOMAS?
SHUT
WOULD YOU LIKE SOME MORE BACON?
HMM...
NO, THANK YOU.
My father did not leave that day, but he did not join us for breakfast.
My aunt and uncle rode unicycles around everything...
... drowning the morning in forced theatrics and sad, knowing smiles.

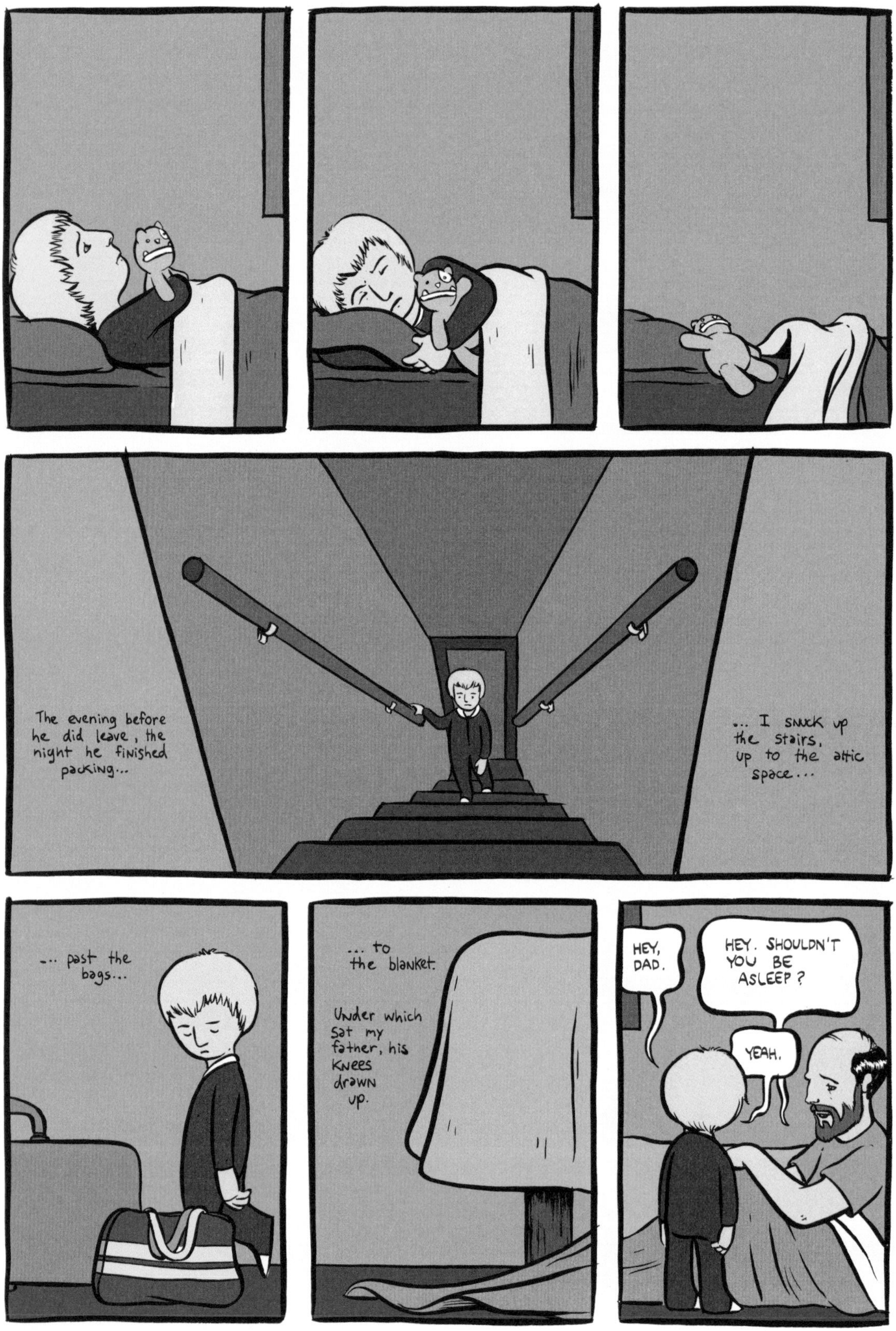
The evening before he did leave, the night he finished packing...
... I snuck up the stairs, up to the attic space...
... past the bags...
... to the blanket.
Under which sat my father, his knees drawn up.
HEY, DAD.
HEY. SHOULDN'T YOU BE ASLEEP?
YEAH.

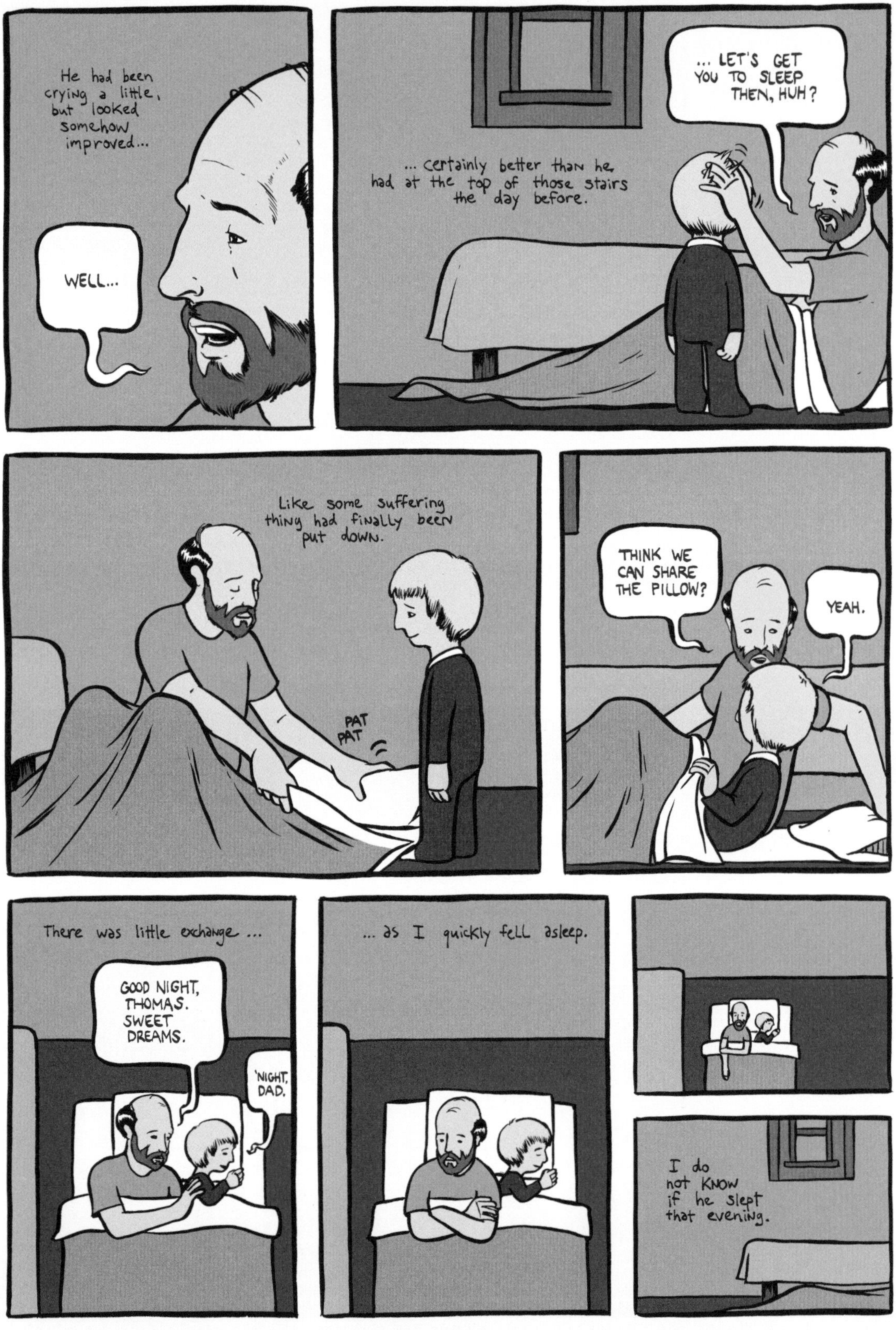
He had been crying a little, but looked somehow improved...
WELL...
... certainly better than he had at the top of those stairs the day before.
... LET'S GET YOU TO SLEEP THEN, HUH?
Like some suffering thing had finally been put down.
PAT PAT
THINK WE CAN SHARE THE PILLOW?
YEAH.
There was little exchange ...
GOOD NIGHT, THOMAS. SWEET DREAMS.
'NIGHT, DAD.
... as I quickly fell asleep.
I do not know if he slept that evening.

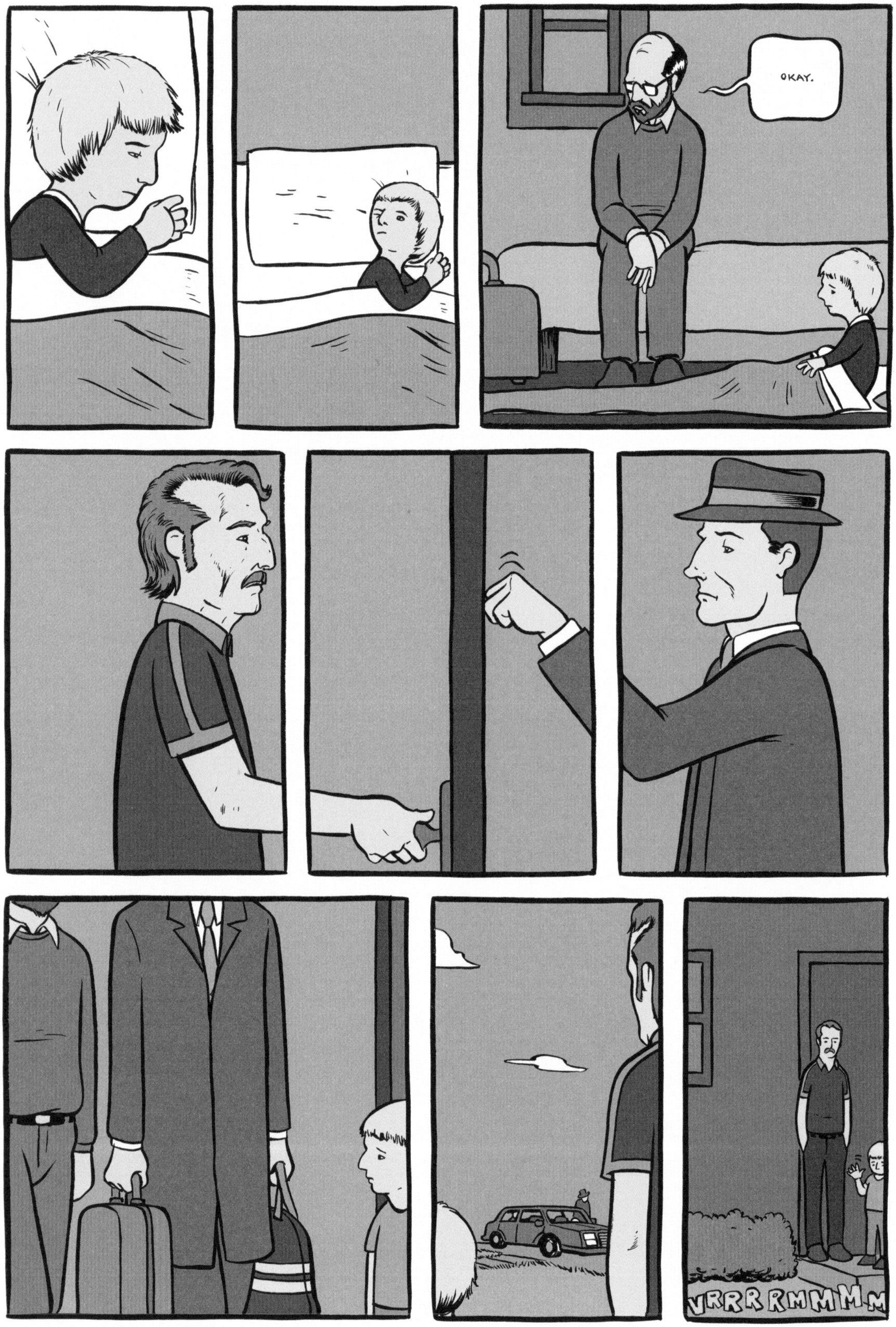
OKAY.
VRRRRMMMMM

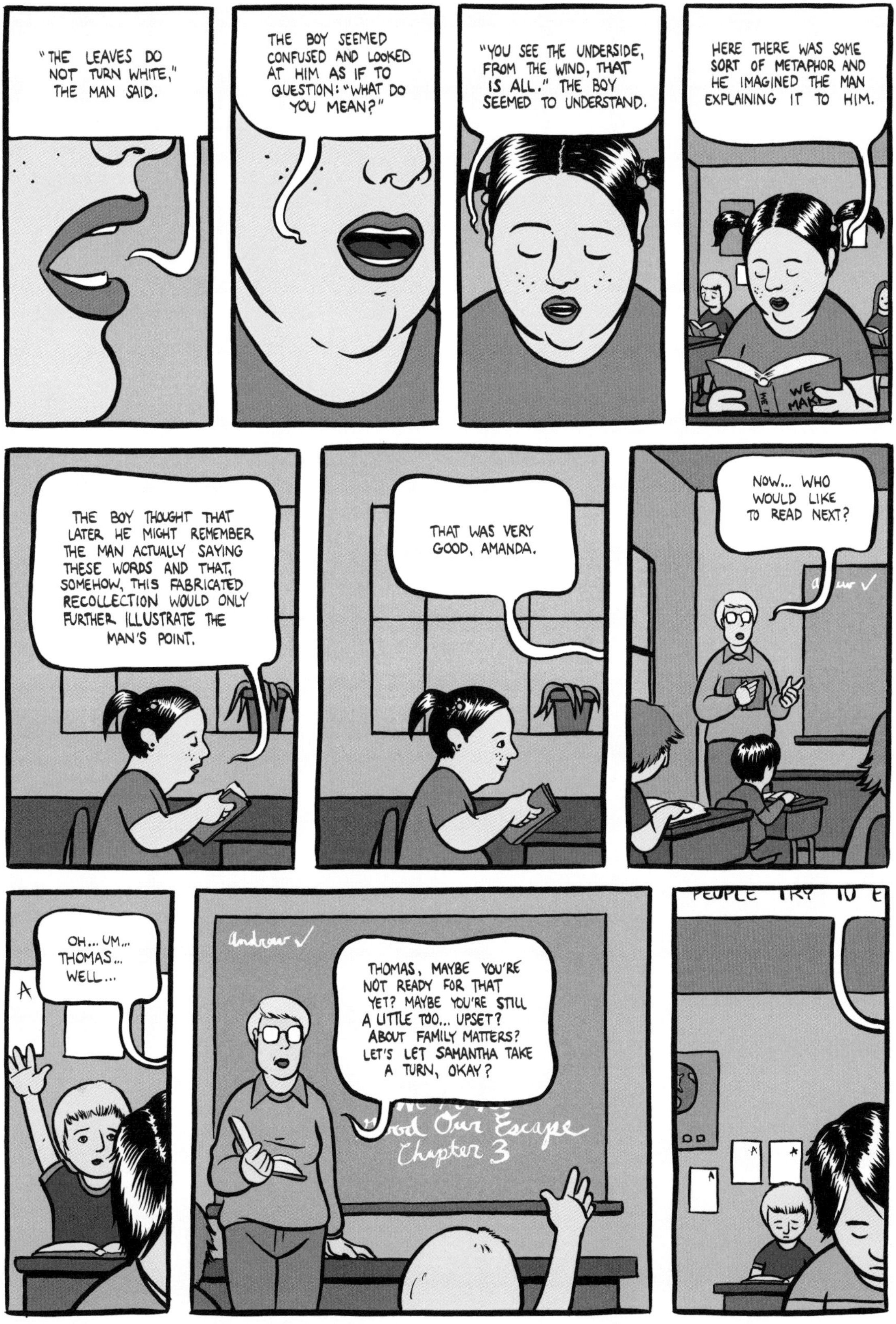
"THE LEAVES DO NOT TURN WHITE," THE MAN SAID.
THE BOY SEEMED CONFUSED AND LOOKED AT HIM AS IF TO QUESTION: "WHAT DO YOU MEAN?"
"YOU SEE THE UNDERSIDE, FROM THE WIND, THAT IS ALL." THE BOY SEEMED TO UNDERSTAND.
HERE THERE WAS SOME SORT OF METAPHOR AND HE IMAGINED THE MAN EXPLAINING IT TO HIM.
THE BOY THOUGHT THAT LATER HE MIGHT REMEMBER THE MAN ACTUALLY SAYING THESE WORDS AND THAT, SOMEHOW, THIS FABRICATED RECOLLECTION WOULD ONLY FURTHER ILLUSTRATE THE MAN'S POINT.
THAT WAS VERY GOOD, AMANDA.
NOW... WHO WOULD LIKE TO READ NEXT?
OH... UM... THOMAS... WELL...
Andrew ✓
THOMAS, MAYBE YOU'RE NOT READY FOR THAT YET? MAYBE YOU'RE STILL A LITTLE TOO... UPSET? ABOUT FAMILY MATTERS? LET'S LET SAMANTHA TAKE A TURN, OKAY?
Chapter 3
PEOPLE TRY TO E

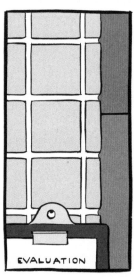

EVALUATION

VERY GOOD. NOW LET'S TRY TO RECALL WHAT YOU WORE TO THE FUNERAL.

WELL, OF COURSE I'VE BEEN TO QUITE A FEW FUNERALS, SO YOU'LL HAVE..

DAVID, YOUR WIFE'S... YOUR WIFE'S FUNERAL.

DAVID?

DAVID?

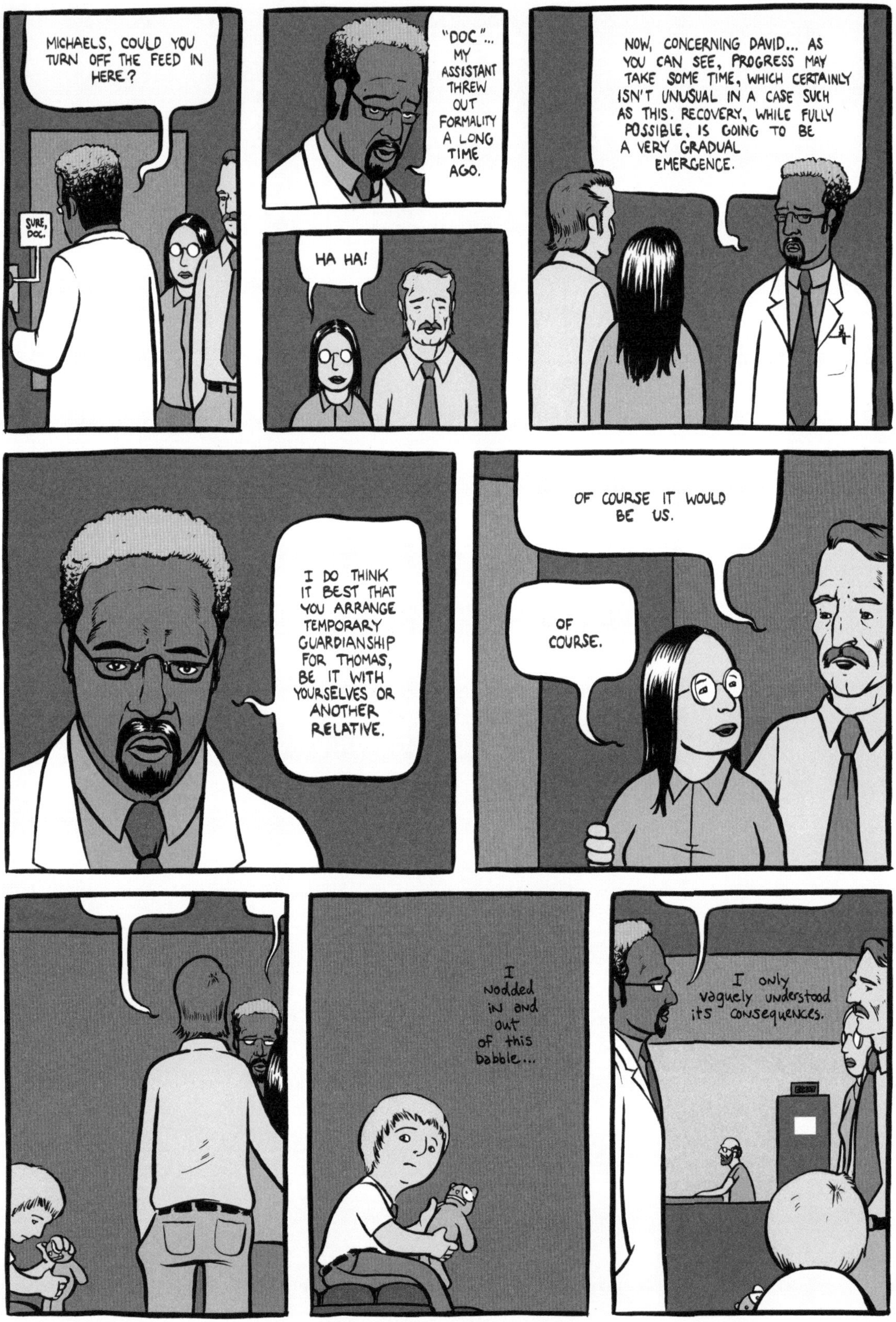
MICHAELS, COULD YOU TURN OFF THE FEED IN HERE?
SURE, DOC.
"DOC"... MY ASSISTANT THREW OUT FORMALITY A LONG TIME AGO.
HA HA!
NOW, CONCERNING DAVID... AS YOU CAN SEE, PROGRESS MAY TAKE SOME TIME, WHICH CERTAINLY ISN'T UNUSUAL IN A CASE SUCH AS THIS. RECOVERY, WHILE FULLY POSSIBLE, IS GOING TO BE A VERY GRADUAL EMERGENCE.
I DO THINK IT BEST THAT YOU ARRANGE TEMPORARY GUARDIANSHIP FOR THOMAS, BE IT WITH YOURSELVES OR ANOTHER RELATIVE.
OF COURSE IT WOULD BE US.
OF COURSE.
I nodded in and out of this babble...
I only vaguely understood its consequences.

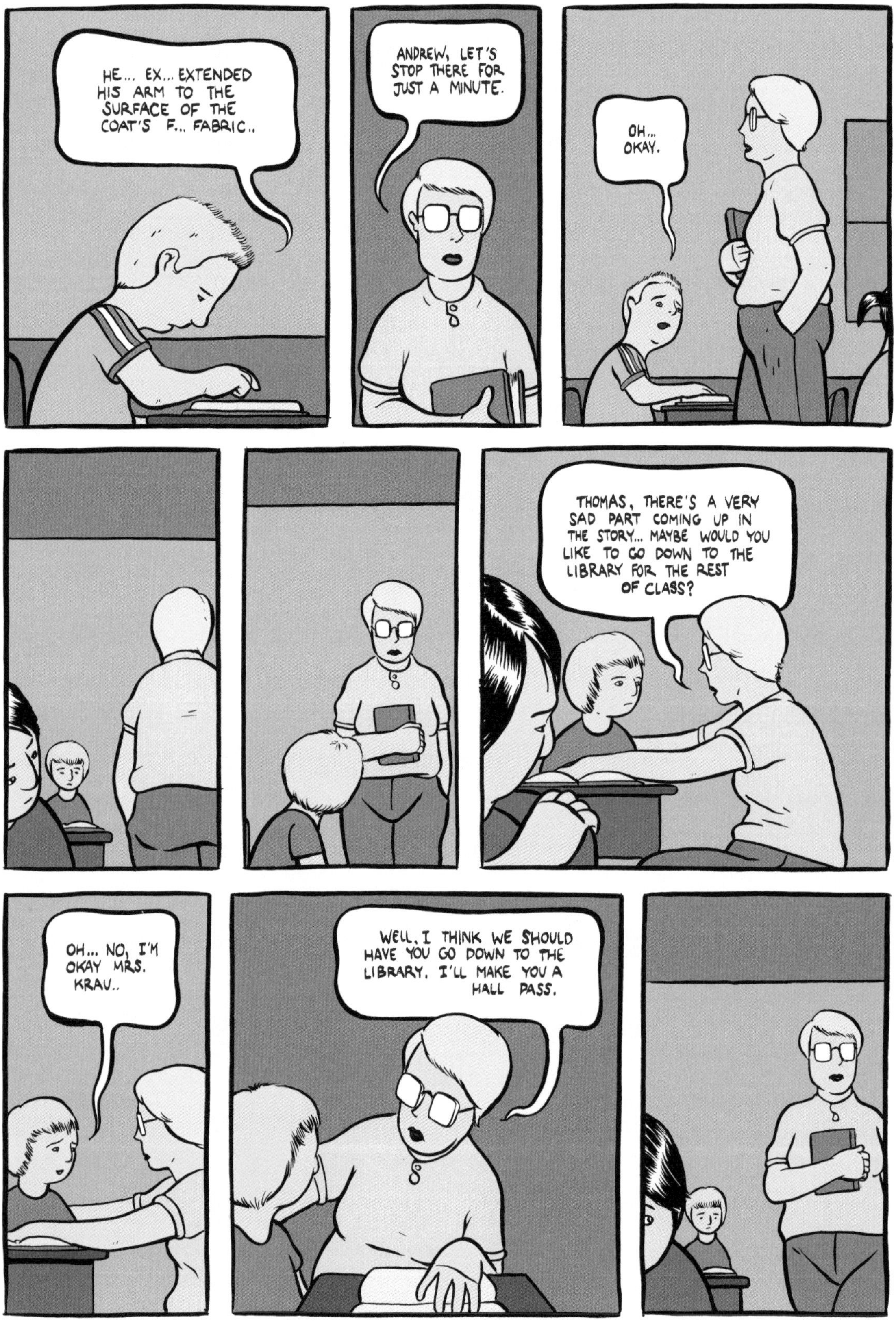
HE... EX... EXTENDED HIS ARM TO THE SURFACE OF THE COAT'S F... FABRIC..
ANDREW, LET'S STOP THERE FOR JUST A MINUTE.
OH... OKAY.
THOMAS, THERE'S A VERY SAD PART COMING UP IN THE STORY... MAYBE WOULD YOU LIKE TO GO DOWN TO THE LIBRARY FOR THE REST OF CLASS?
OH... NO, I'M OKAY MRS. KRAU..
WELL, I THINK WE SHOULD HAVE YOU GO DOWN TO THE LIBRARY. I'LL MAKE YOU A HALL PASS.

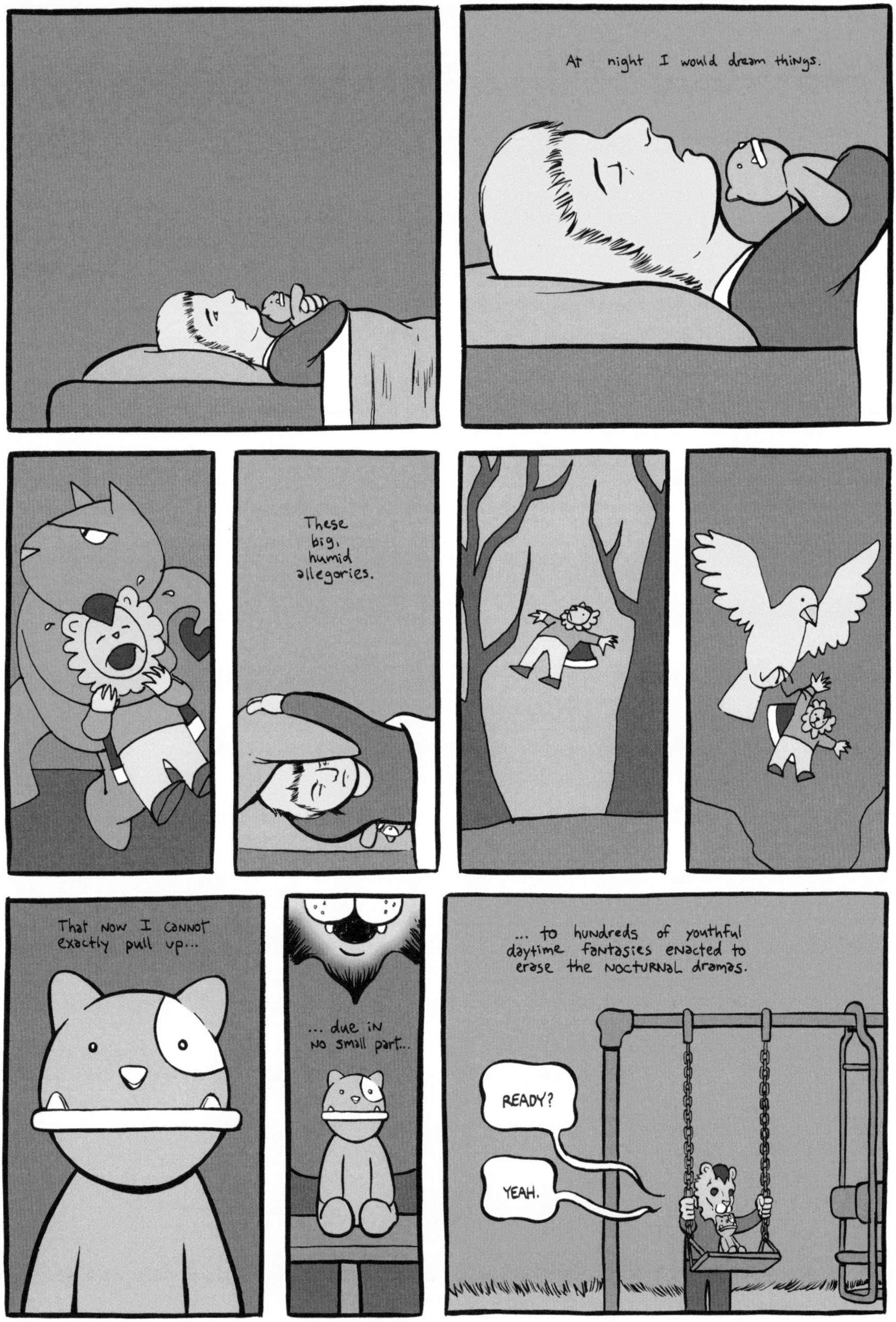
At night I would dream things.
These big, humid allegories.
That now I cannot exactly pull up...
... due in no small part...
... to hundreds of youthful daytime fantasies enacted to erase the nocturnal dramas.
READY?
YEAH.

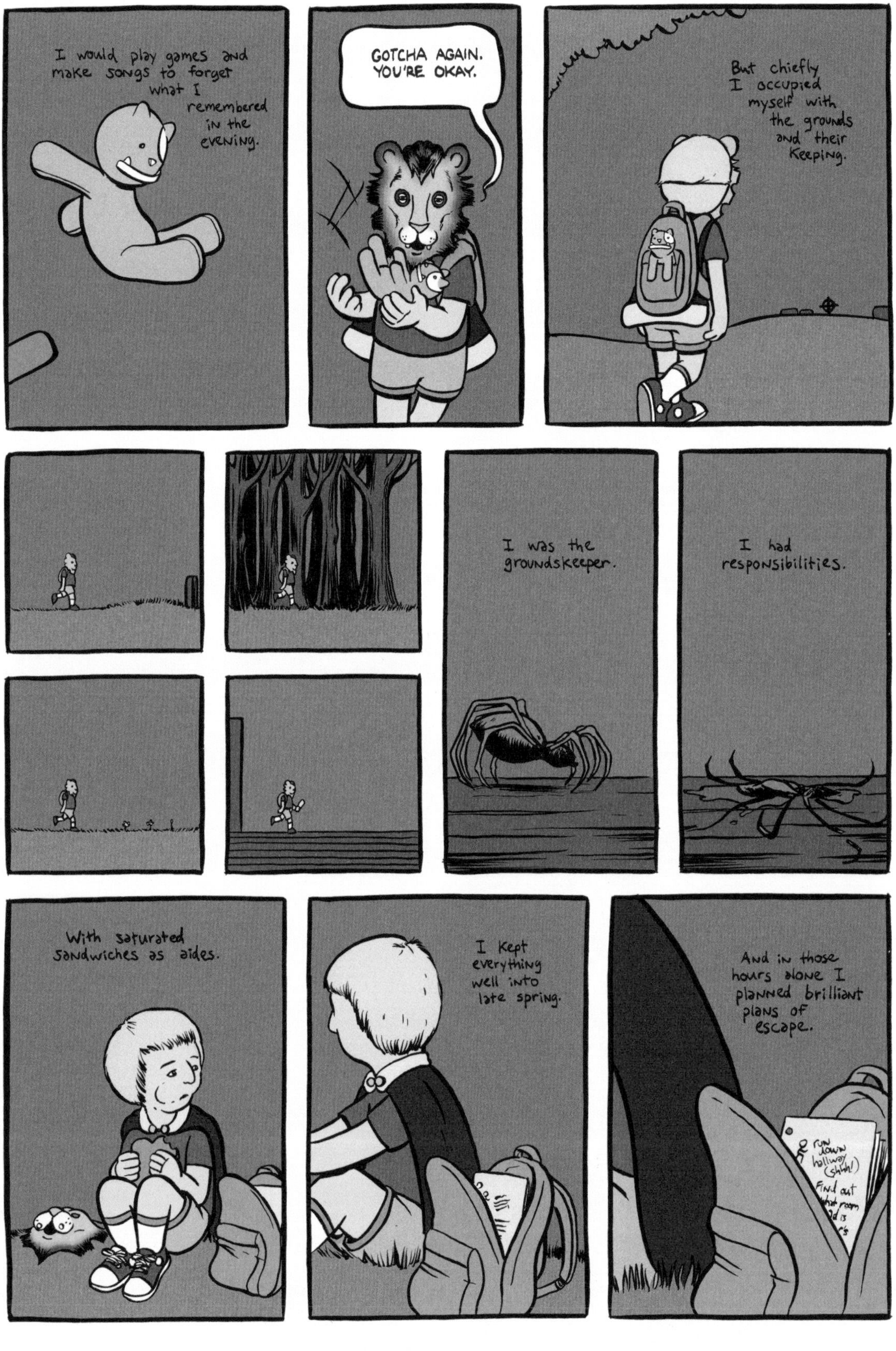
I would play games and make songs to forget what I remembered in the evening.
GOTCHA AGAIN. YOU'RE OKAY.
But chiefly I occupied myself with the grounds and their keeping.
I was the groundskeeper.
I had responsibilities.
With saturated sandwiches as aides.
I kept everything well into late spring.
And in those hours alone I planned brilliant plans of escape.
run down hallway (shhh!)
Find out

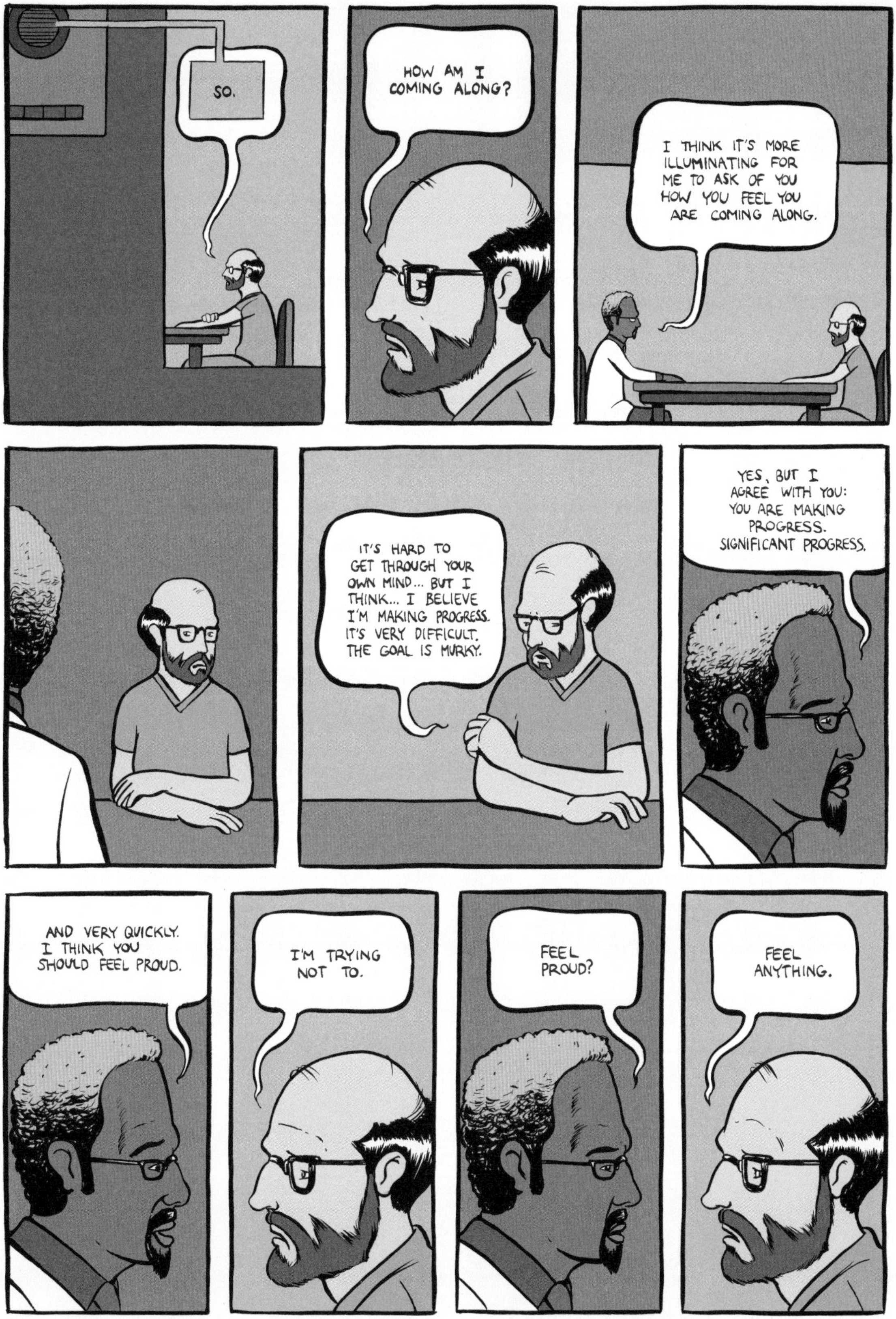
SO.
HOW AM I COMING ALONG?
I THINK IT'S MORE ILLUMINATING FOR ME TO ASK OF YOU HOW YOU FEEL YOU ARE COMING ALONG.
IT'S HARD TO GET THROUGH YOUR OWN MIND... BUT I THINK... I BELIEVE I'M MAKING PROGRESS. IT'S VERY DIFFICULT. THE GOAL IS MURKY.
YES, BUT I AGREE WITH YOU: YOU ARE MAKING PROGRESS. SIGNIFICANT PROGRESS.
AND VERY QUICKLY. I THINK YOU SHOULD FEEL PROUD.
I'M TRYING NOT TO.
FEEL PROUD?
FEEL ANYTHING.

WELL, I... IT'S HUMAN TO FEEL THESE THINGS, DAVID... PRIDE AT ACCOMPLISHMENT, EMPTINESS FROM LOSS... IT'S JUST THAT WE HAVE TO KEEP AN ANCHOR IN REALITY.

IT'S WHEN WE LOSE OURSELVES IN THE FEELINGS - WHEN WE PULL UP ANCHOR, SO TO SPEAK - THAT WE ENDANGER OURSELVES AND THE ONES FOR WHOM WE CARE.

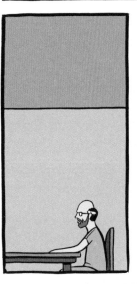

COUGH

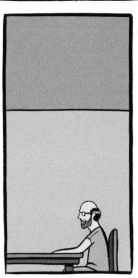

SHE'S DEAD.

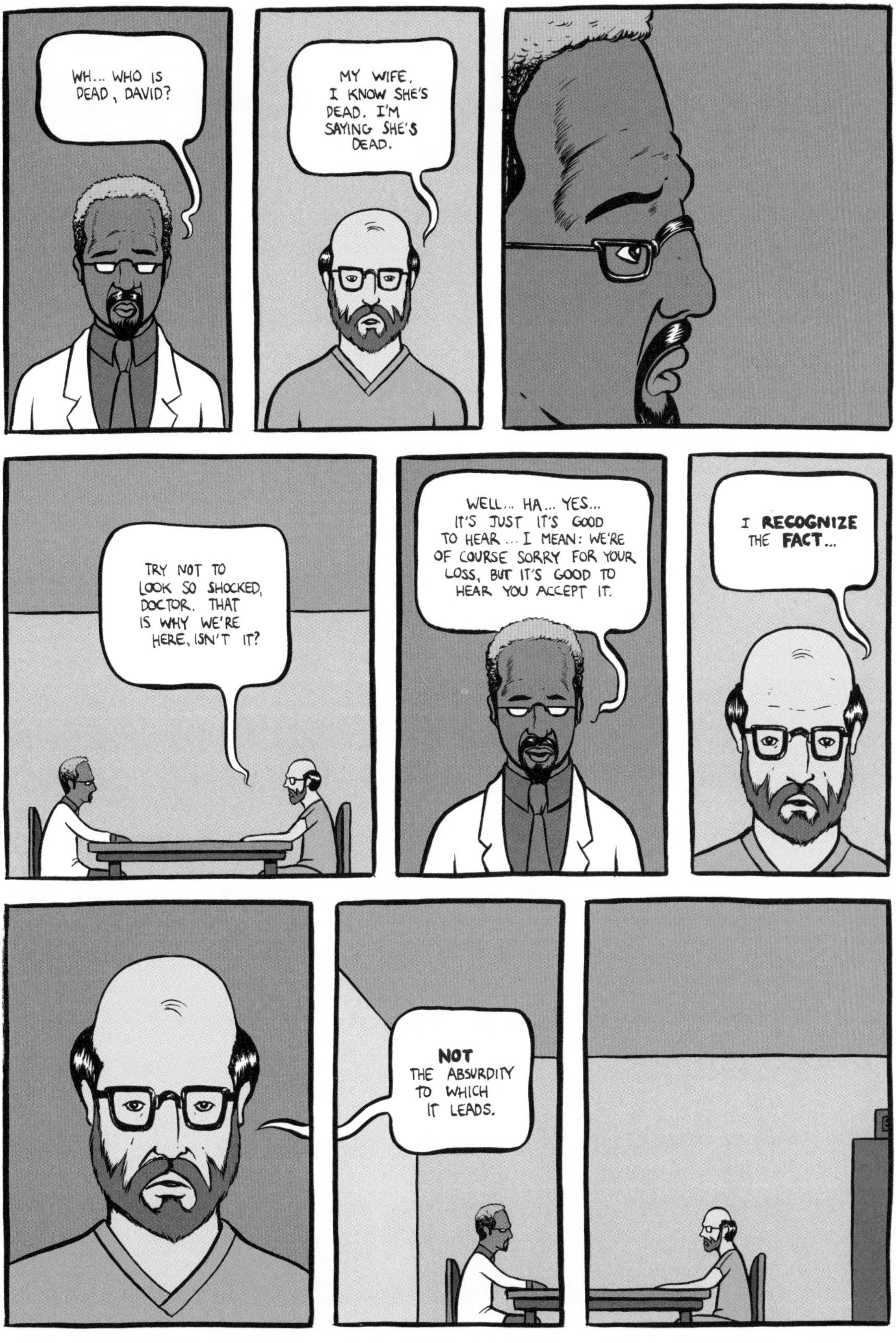
WH... WHO IS DEAD, DAVID?
MY WIFE. I KNOW SHE'S DEAD. I'M SAYING SHE'S DEAD.
TRY NOT TO LOOK SO SHOCKED, DOCTOR. THAT IS WHY WE'RE HERE, ISN'T IT?
WELL... HA... YES... IT'S JUST IT'S GOOD TO HEAR ... I MEAN: WE'RE OF COURSE SORRY FOR YOUR LOSS, BUT IT'S GOOD TO HEAR YOU ACCEPT IT.
I **RECOGNIZE** THE **FACT**...
NOT THE ABSURDITY TO WHICH IT LEADS.

THE GARDEN REVISED

The grass had grown up thick over her.

The old garden was dark with muddy, wilting things that I could not bring back.

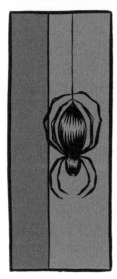

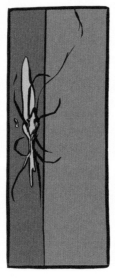

Slowly I elected the flourishing grass her new garden and forcefully forgot the dark patch of land.

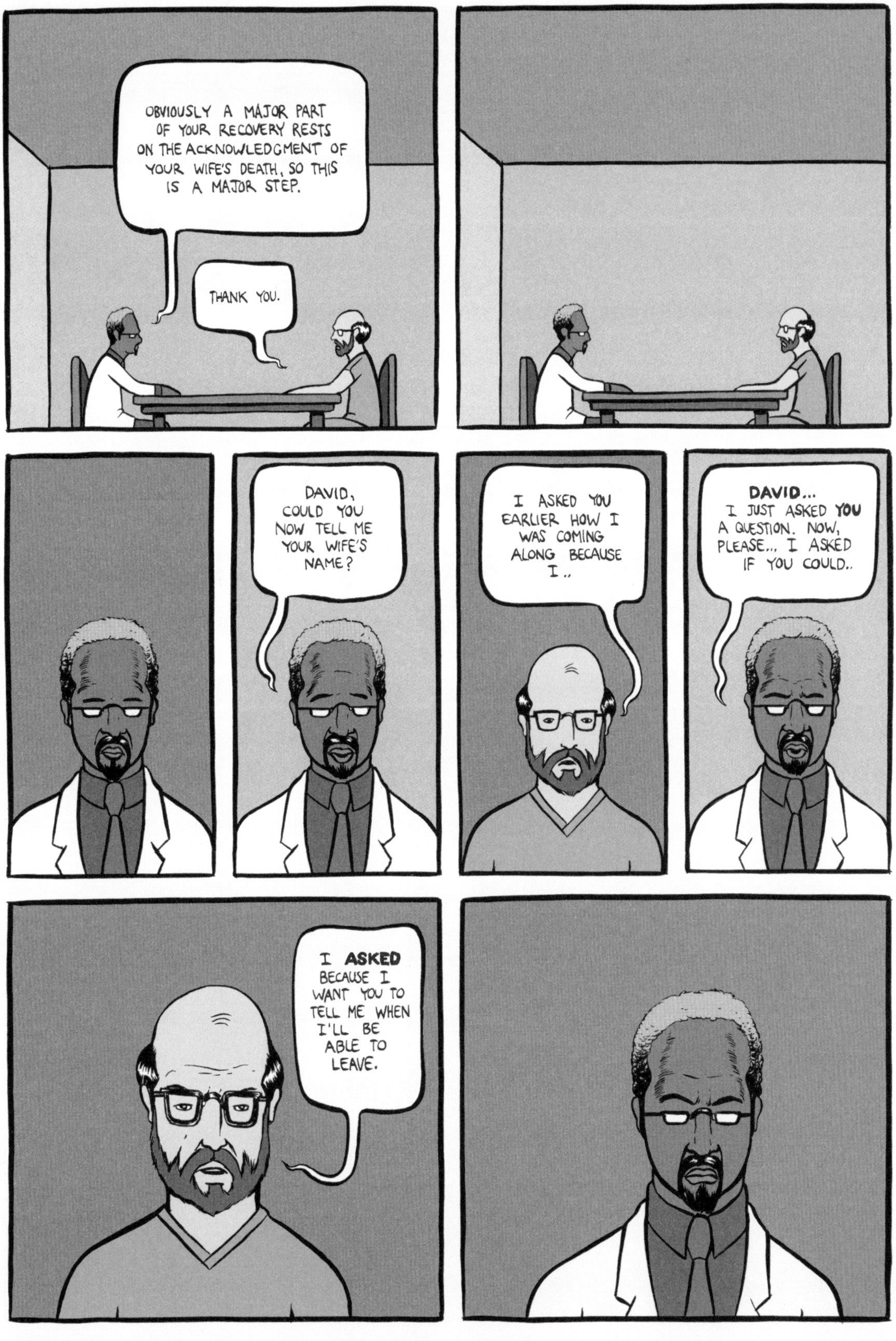
OBVIOUSLY A MAJOR PART OF YOUR RECOVERY RESTS ON THE ACKNOWLEDGMENT OF YOUR WIFE'S DEATH, SO THIS IS A MAJOR STEP.
THANK YOU.
DAVID, COULD YOU NOW TELL ME YOUR WIFE'S NAME?
I ASKED YOU EARLIER HOW I WAS COMING ALONG BECAUSE I..
DAVID... I JUST ASKED YOU A QUESTION. NOW, PLEASE... I ASKED IF YOU COULD..
I ASKED BECAUSE I WANT YOU TO TELL ME WHEN I'LL BE ABLE TO LEAVE.

YOU ARE HERE VOLUNTARILY, DAVID... YOU KNOW YOU CAN RELEASE YOURSELF AT ANY TIME.

OF COURSE, IT IS IN YOUR BEST INTERESTS, IN REGARD TO MAINTAINING GUARDIANSHIP OF YOUR SON, TO MAKE SURE THE STAFF AND I SUPPORT YOUR RELEASE.

I **MEANT** WHEN DO **YOU** THINK I'LL BE READY.

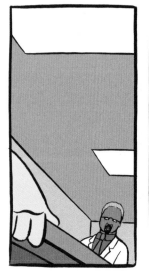

I'M NOT SURE THAT'S SOMETHING I CAN ANSWER JUST YET.

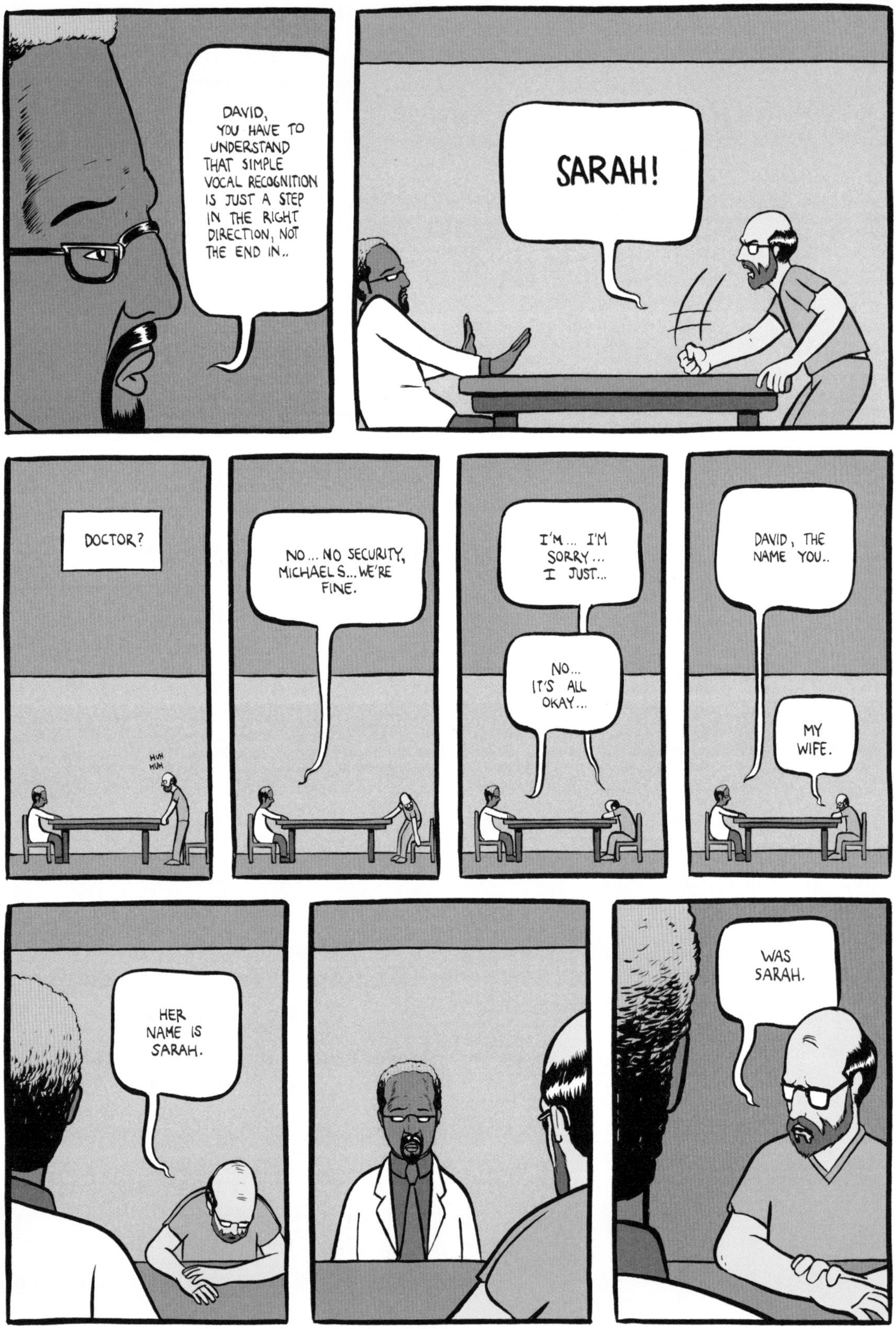
DAVID, YOU HAVE TO UNDERSTAND THAT SIMPLE VOCAL RECOGNITION IS JUST A STEP IN THE RIGHT DIRECTION, NOT THE END IN..
SARAH!
DOCTOR?
HUH HUH
NO... NO SECURITY, MICHAELS... WE'RE FINE.
I'M... I'M SORRY... I JUST...
NO... IT'S ALL OKAY...
DAVID, THE NAME YOU..
MY WIFE.
HER NAME IS SARAH.
WAS SARAH.

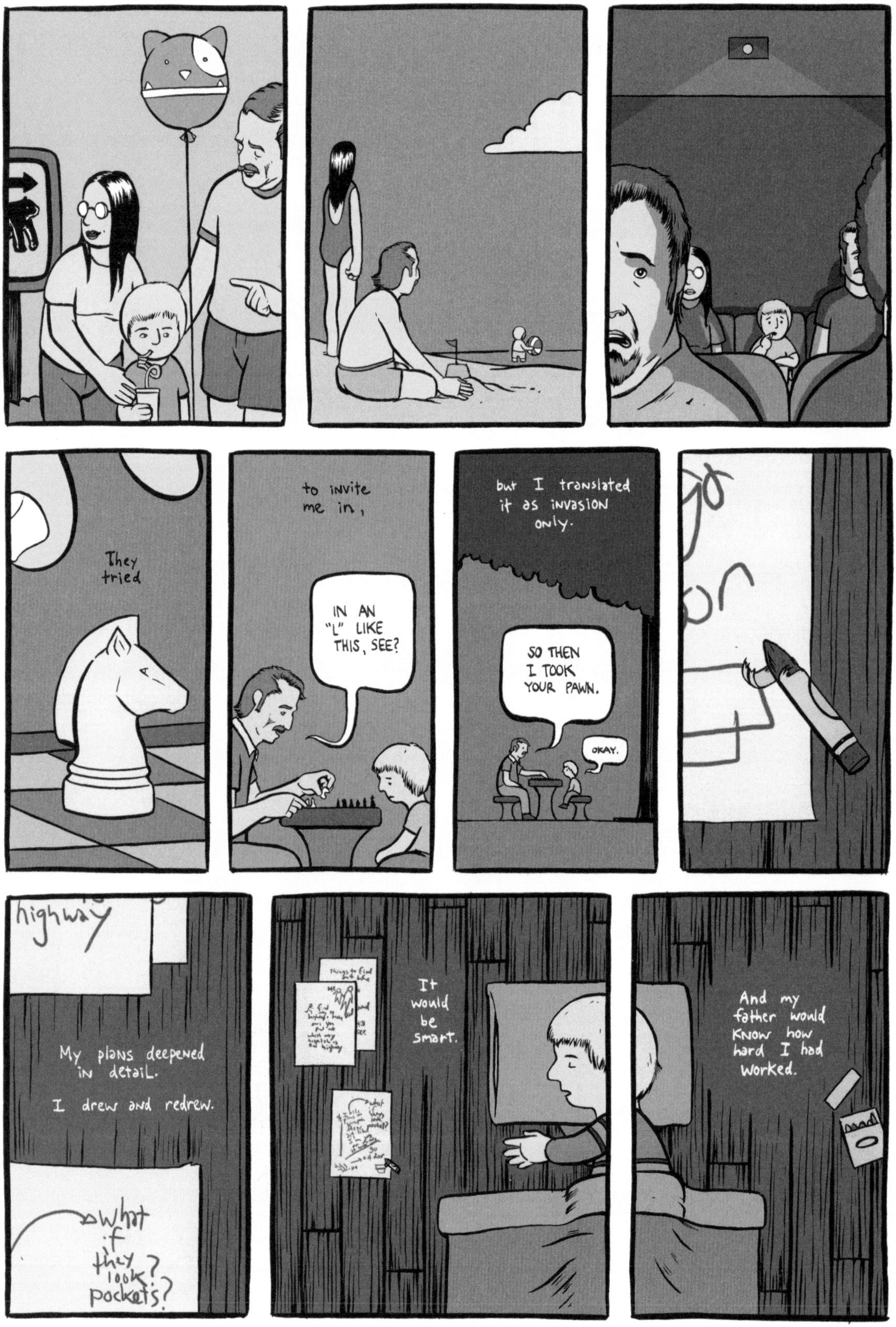

They tried
to invite me in,
IN AN "L" LIKE THIS, SEE?
but I translated it as invasion only.
SO THEN I TOOK YOUR PAWN.
OKAY.
highway
My plans deepened in detail.
I drew and redrew.
what if they look pockets?
It would be smart.
And my father would know how hard I had worked.

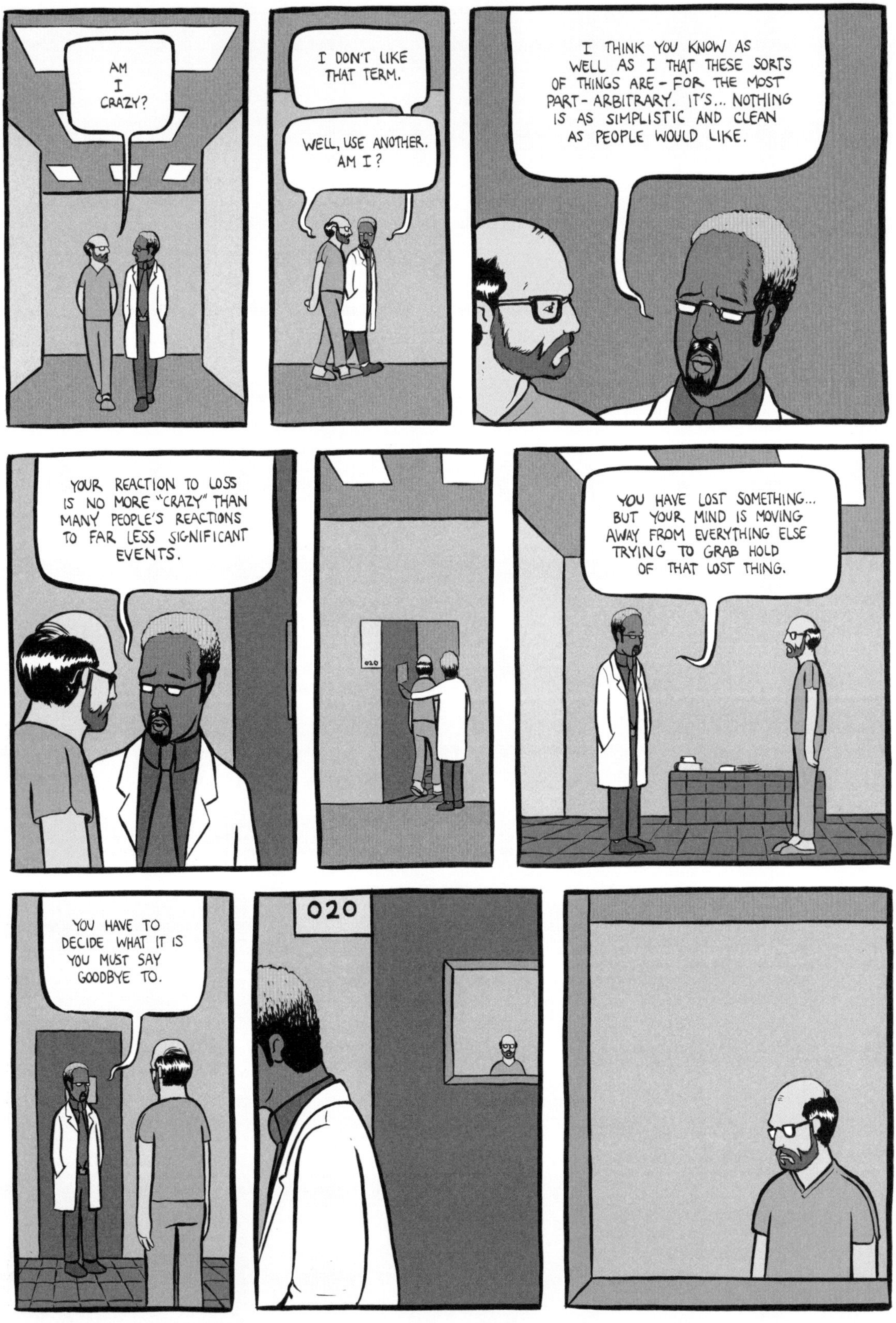
AM I CRAZY?
I DON'T LIKE THAT TERM.
WELL, USE ANOTHER. AM I?
I THINK YOU KNOW AS WELL AS I THAT THESE SORTS OF THINGS ARE - FOR THE MOST PART - ARBITRARY. IT'S... NOTHING IS AS SIMPLISTIC AND CLEAN AS PEOPLE WOULD LIKE.
YOUR REACTION TO LOSS IS NO MORE "CRAZY" THAN MANY PEOPLE'S REACTIONS TO FAR LESS SIGNIFICANT EVENTS.
020
YOU HAVE LOST SOMETHING... BUT YOUR MIND IS MOVING AWAY FROM EVERYTHING ELSE TRYING TO GRAB HOLD OF THAT LOST THING.
YOU HAVE TO DECIDE WHAT IT IS YOU MUST SAY GOODBYE TO.
020

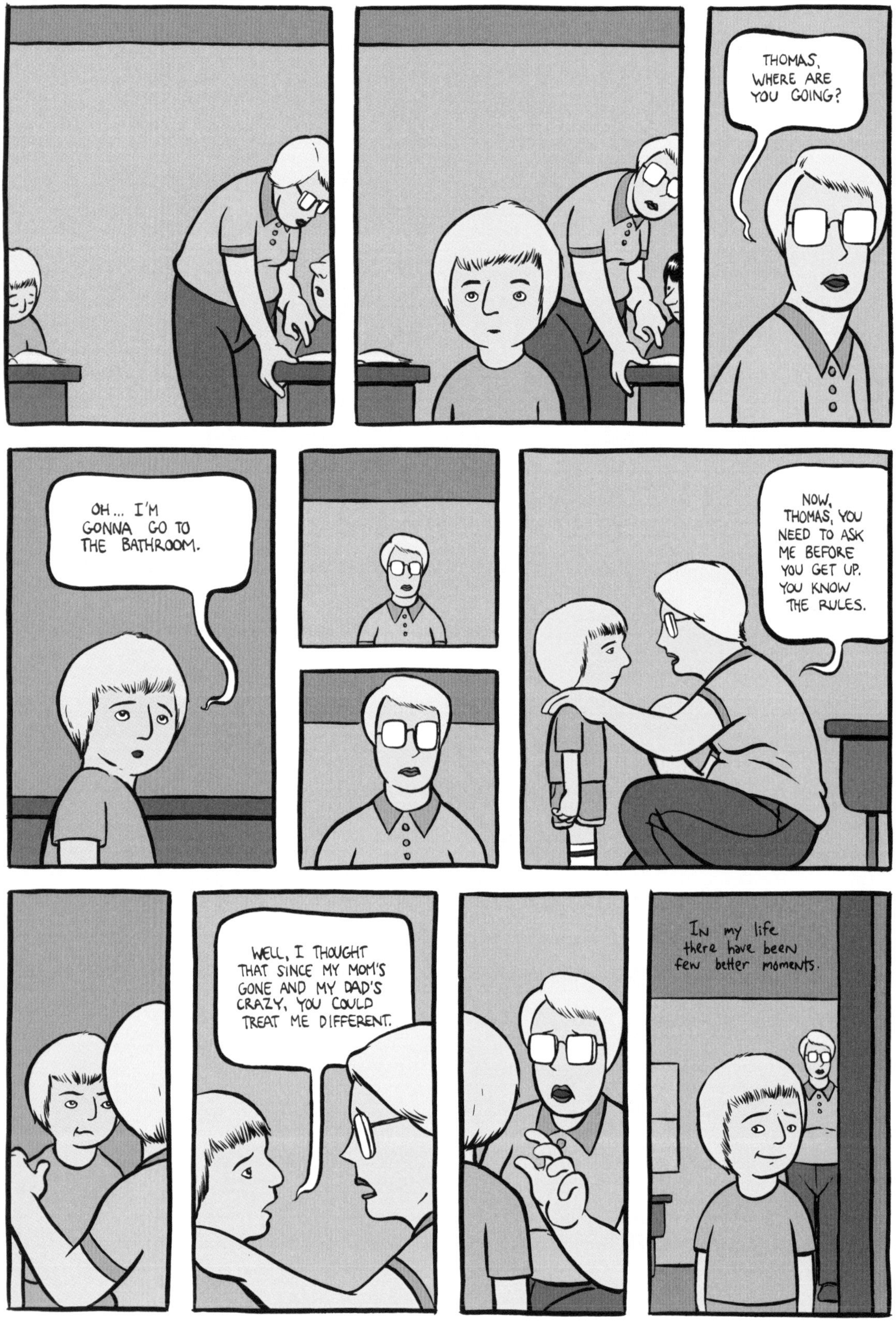
THOMAS, WHERE ARE YOU GOING?
OH... I'M GONNA GO TO THE BATHROOM.
NOW, THOMAS, YOU NEED TO ASK ME BEFORE YOU GET UP. YOU KNOW THE RULES.
WELL, I THOUGHT THAT SINCE MY MOM'S GONE AND MY DAD'S CRAZY, YOU COULD TREAT ME DIFFERENT.
In my life there have been few better moments.

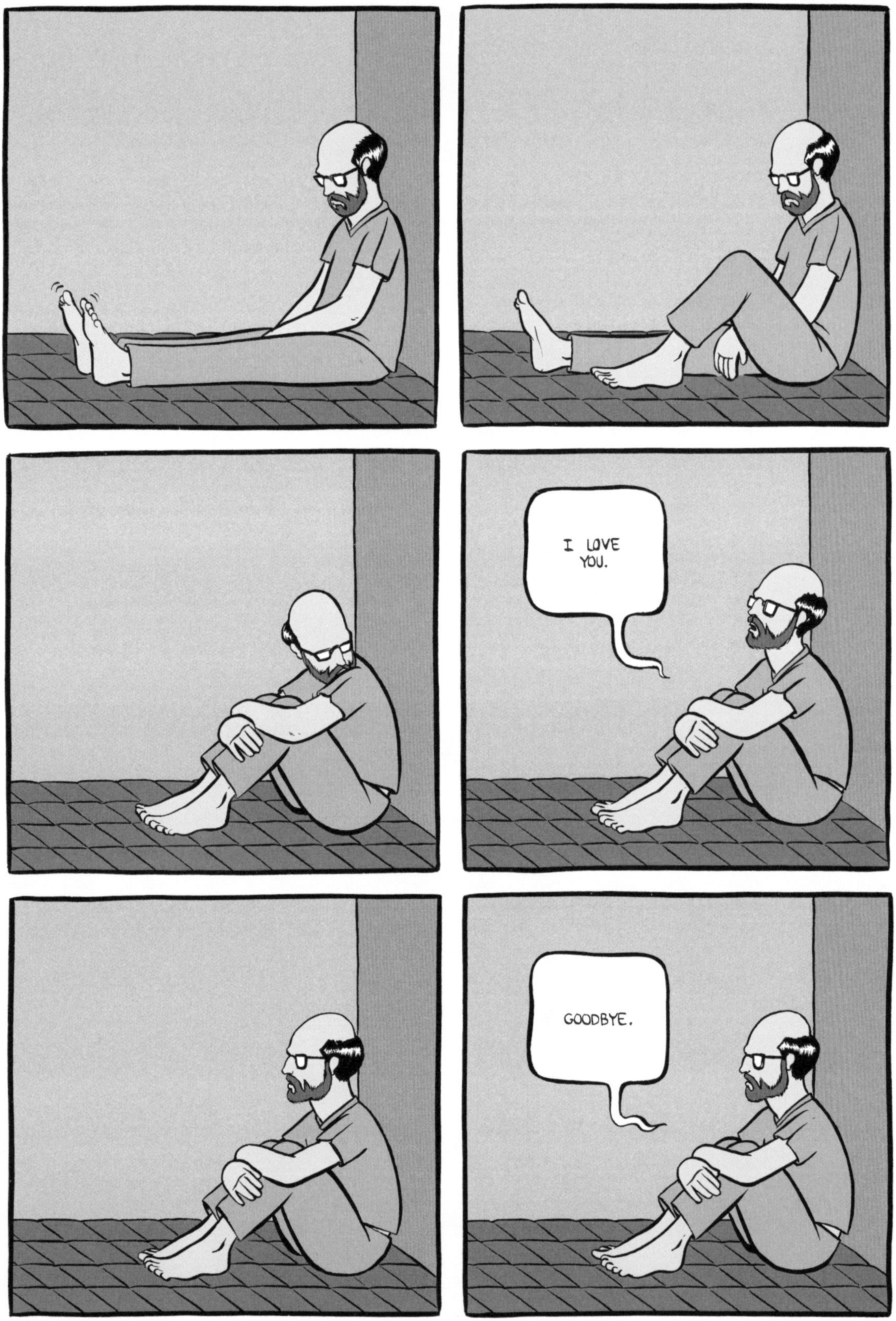
I LOVE YOU.
GOODBYE.

The overthrow of Mrs. Kraufelt, while tremendous and liberating...

... was brief and not without negative consequences.

My uncle and aunt scolded me admirably.

Theirs really was an impossible predicament: to discipline the one thing after whose trust they so sorely pined.

They were of course ignorant of my complete apathy.

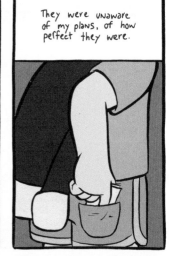
They were unaware of my plans, of how perfect they were.

I walked into the muggy purple-black of that late spring evening...

... knowing they would assume it to be one of my normal rounds.

HOW ARE THE NEW GLASSES?

REALLY GREAT!

Knowing they would not stop me.

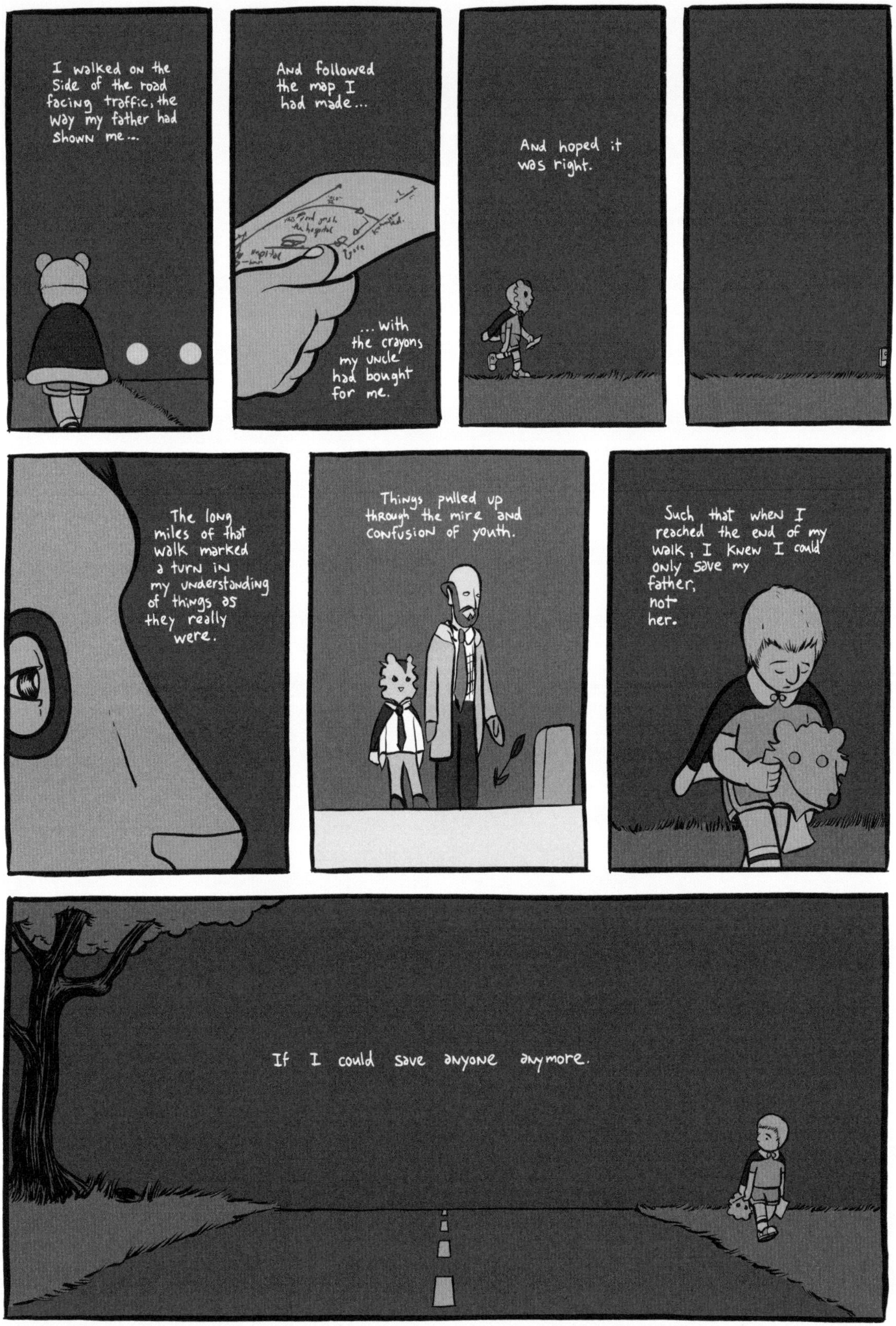
I walked on the side of the road facing traffic, the way my father had shown me...
And followed the map I had made...
...with the crayons my uncle had bought for me.
And hoped it was right.
The long miles of that walk marked a turn in my understanding of things as they really were.
Things pulled up through the mire and confusion of youth.
Such that when I reached the end of my walk, I knew I could only save my father, not her.
If I could save anyone anymore.

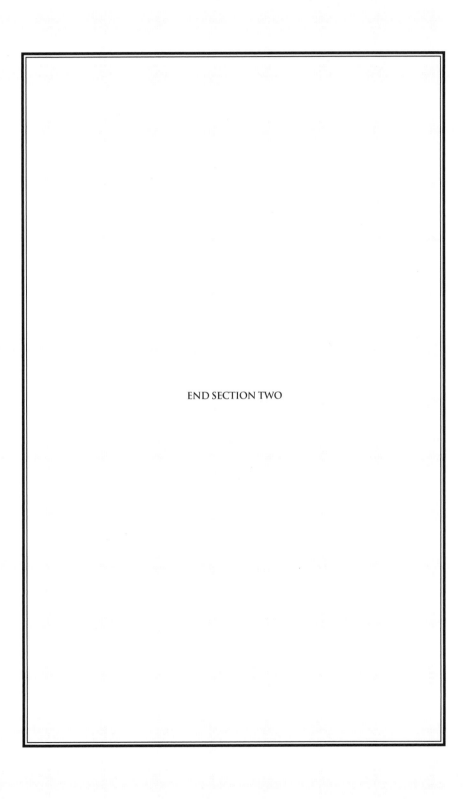

END SECTION TWO

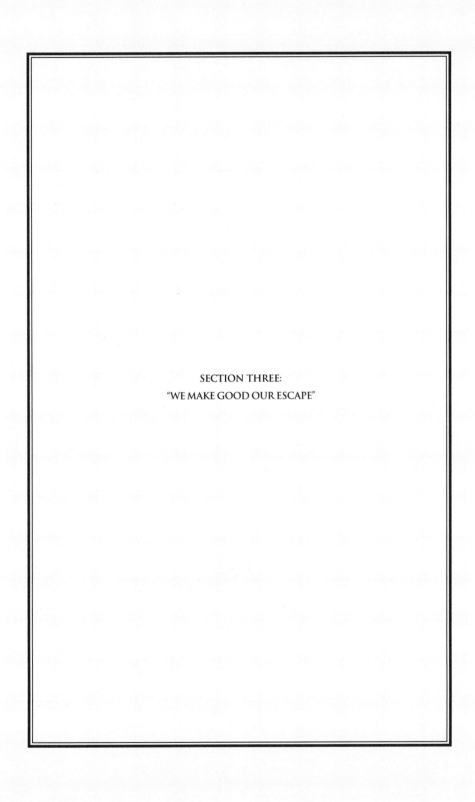

SECTION THREE:
"WE MAKE GOOD OUR ESCAPE"

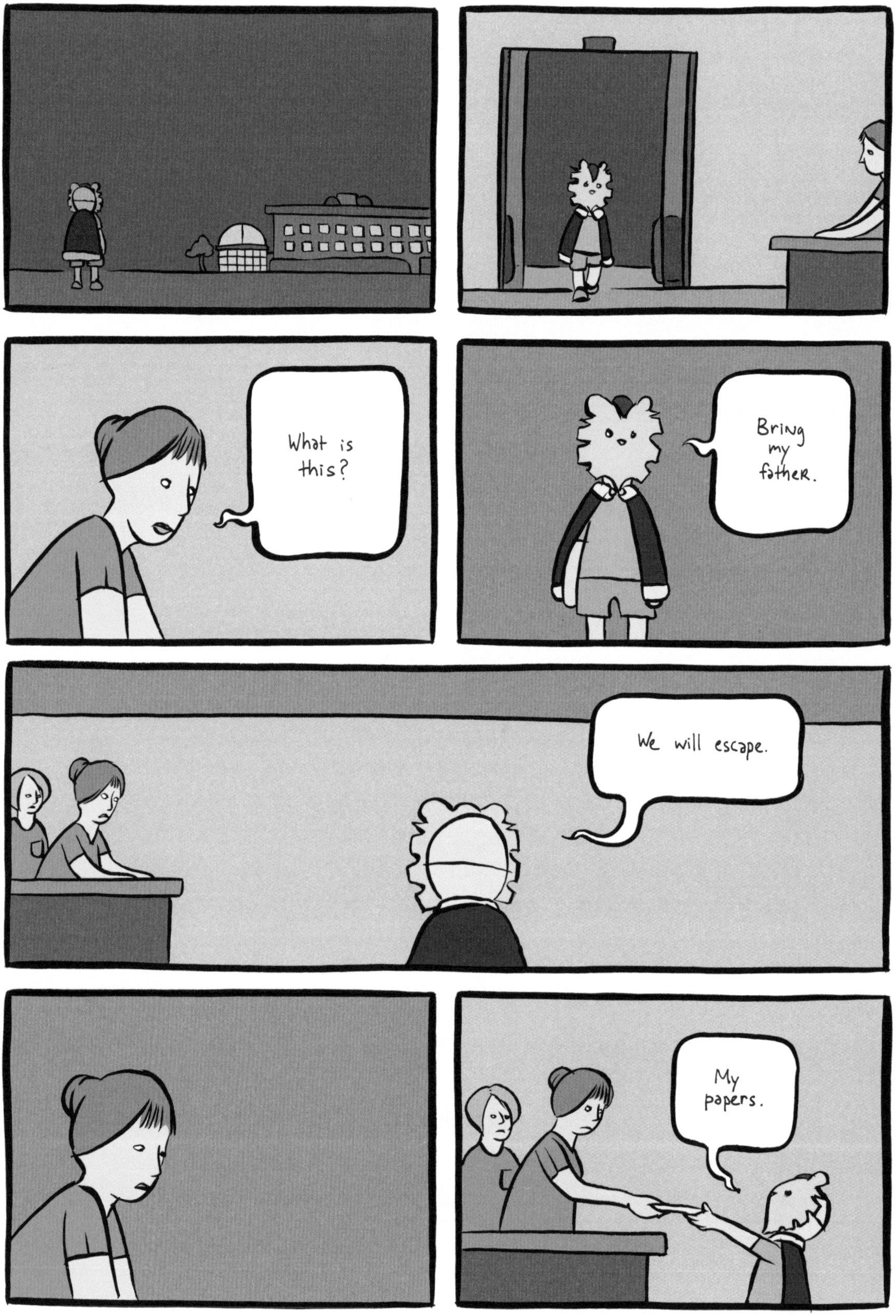
What is this?
Bring my father.
We will escape.
My papers.

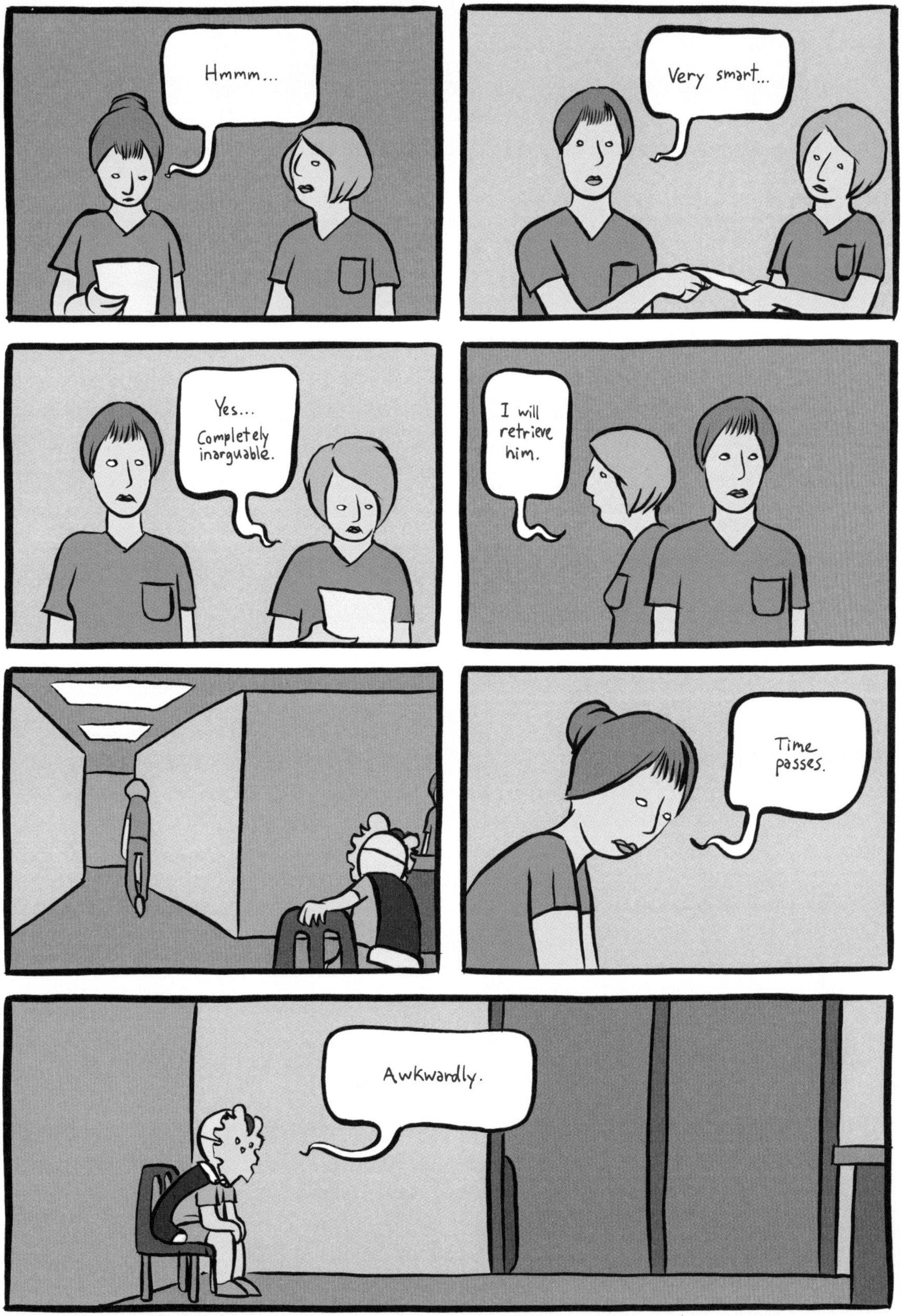
Hmmm...
Very smart...
Yes... Completely inarguable.
I will retrieve him.
Time passes.
Awkwardly.

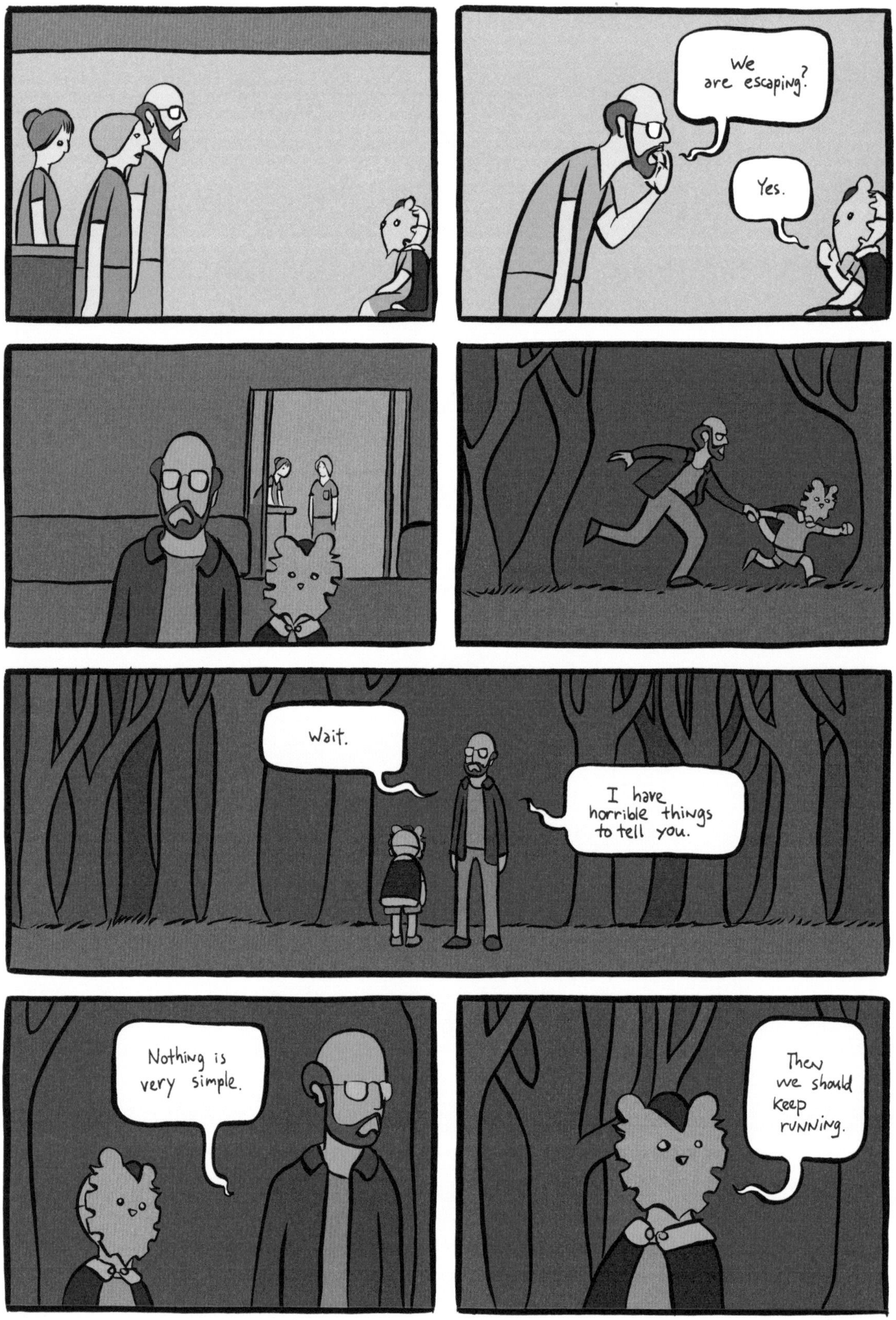
We are escaping?
Yes.
Wait.
I have horrible things to tell you.
Nothing is very simple.
Then we should keep running.

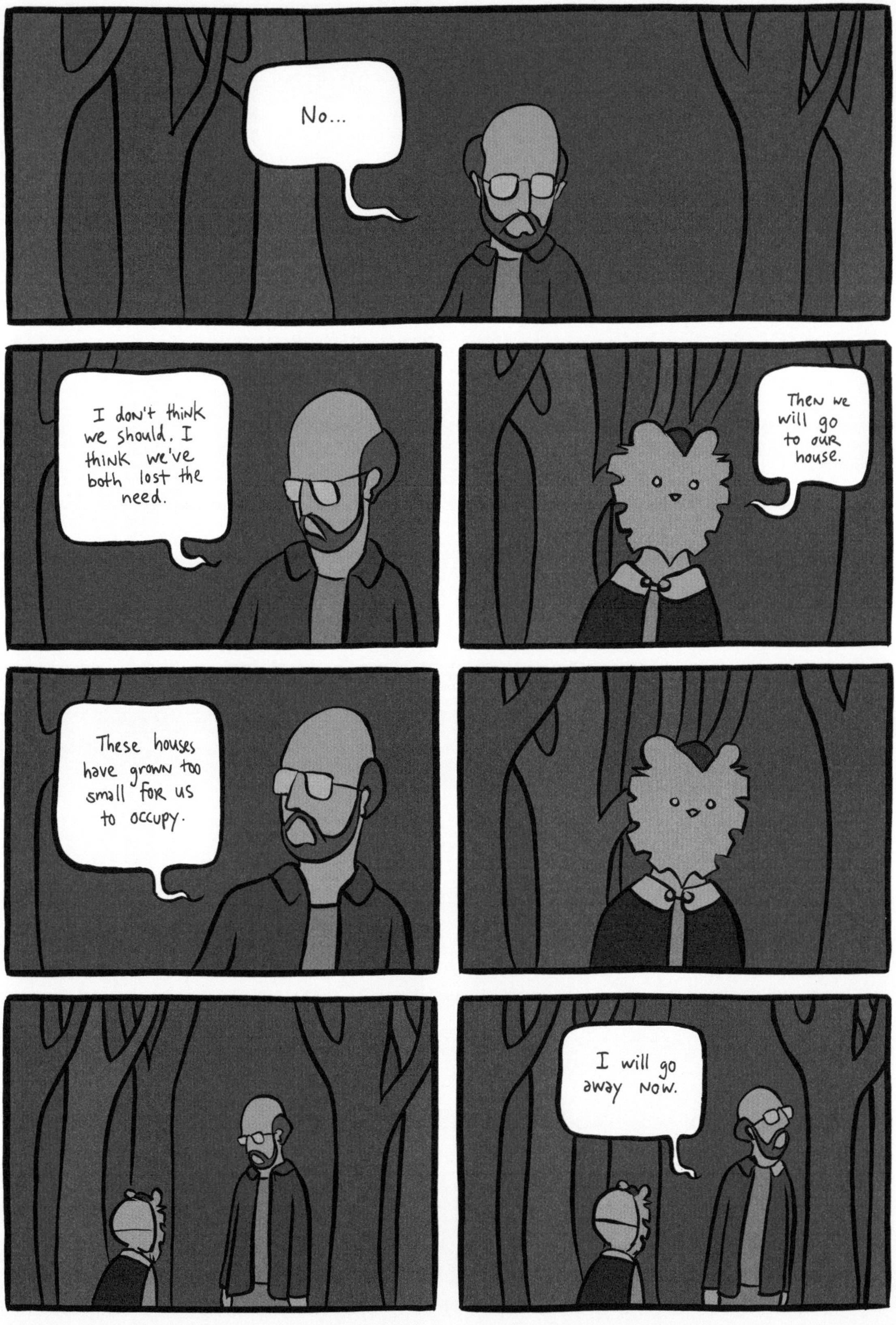
No...
I don't think we should. I think we've both lost the need.
Then we will go to our house.
These houses have grown too small for us to occupy.
I will go away now.

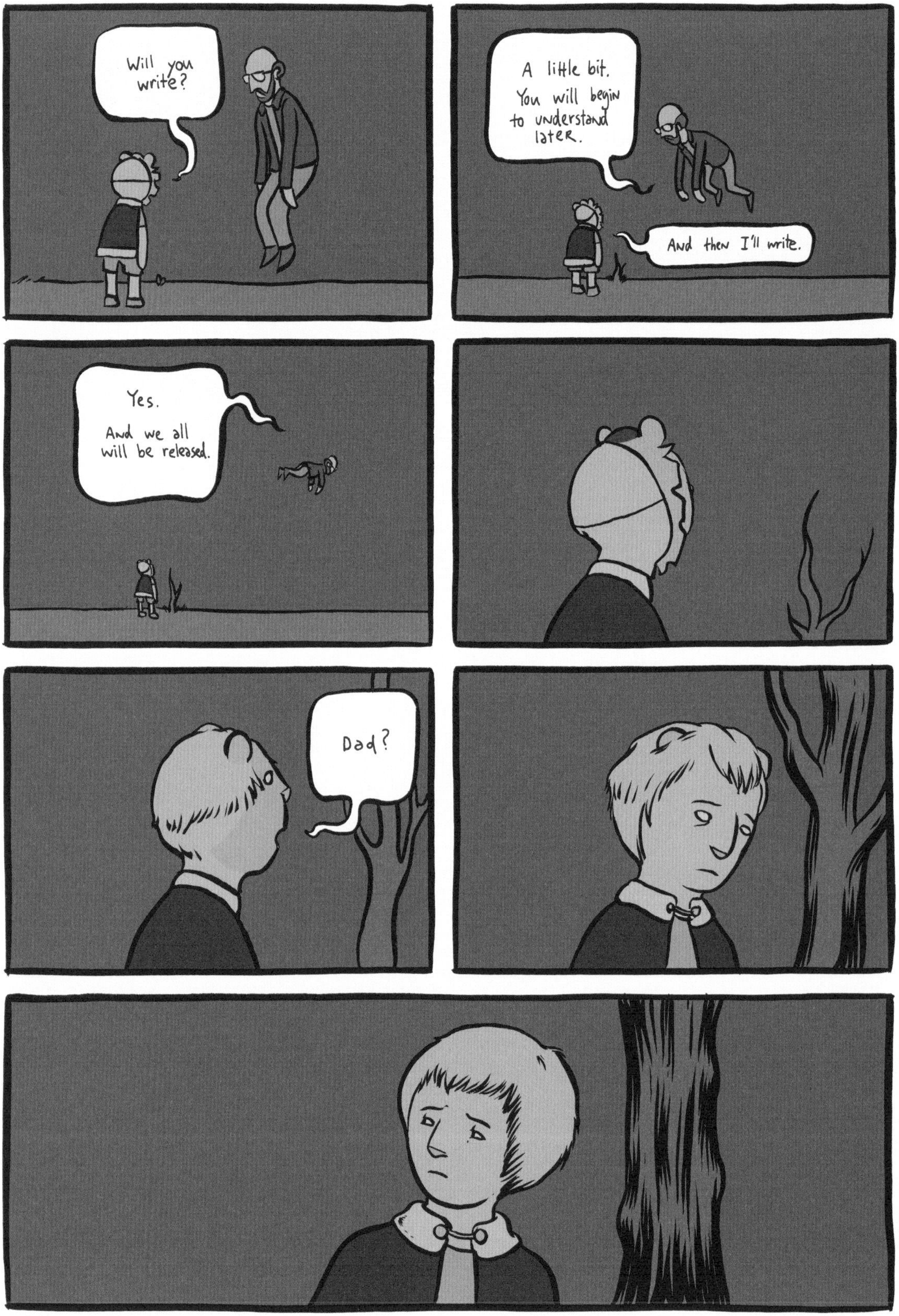
Will you write?
A little bit. You will begin to understand later.
And then I'll write.
Yes. And we all will be released.
Dad?

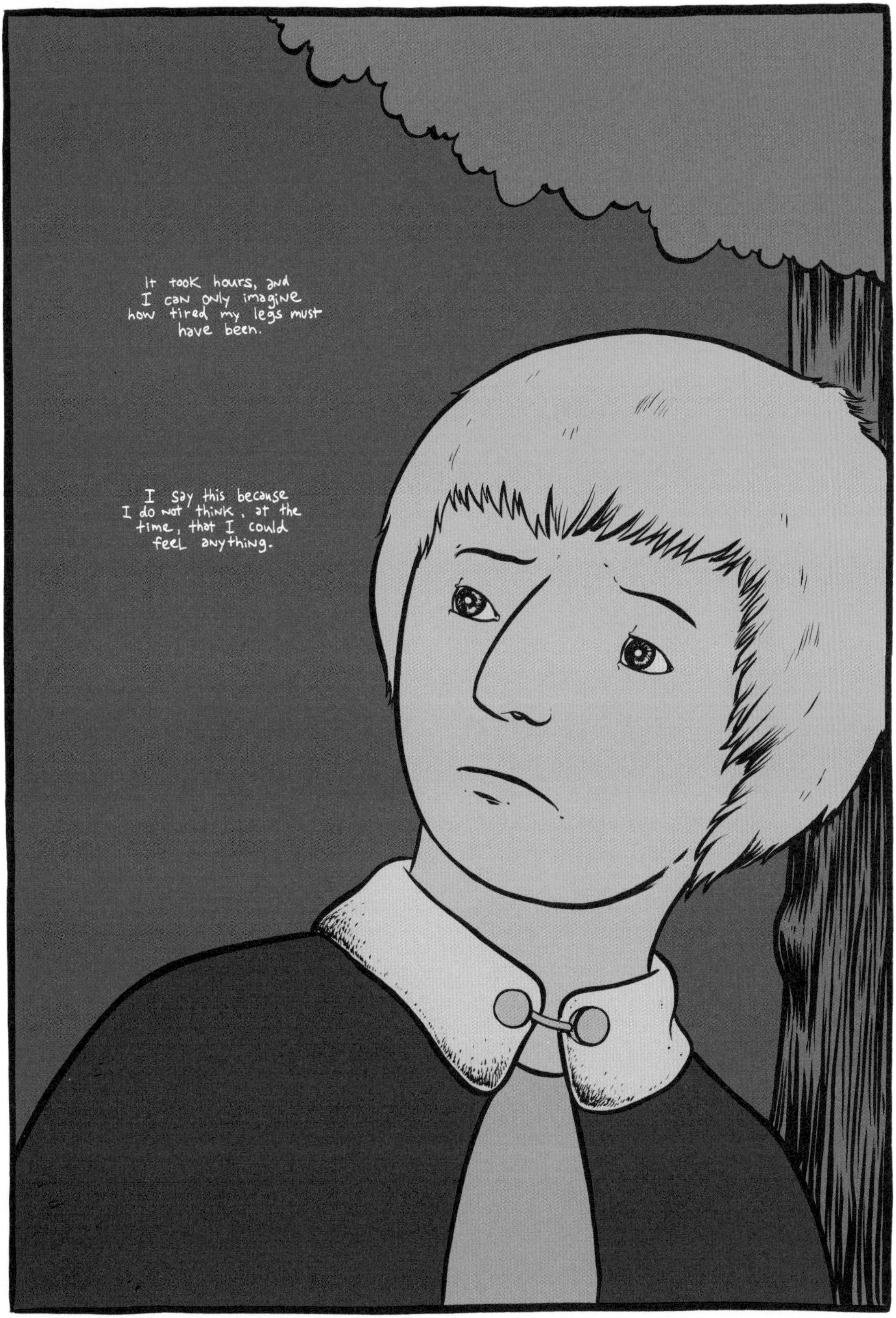
It took hours, and I can only imagine how tired my legs must have been.
I say this because I do not think, at the time, that I could feel anything.

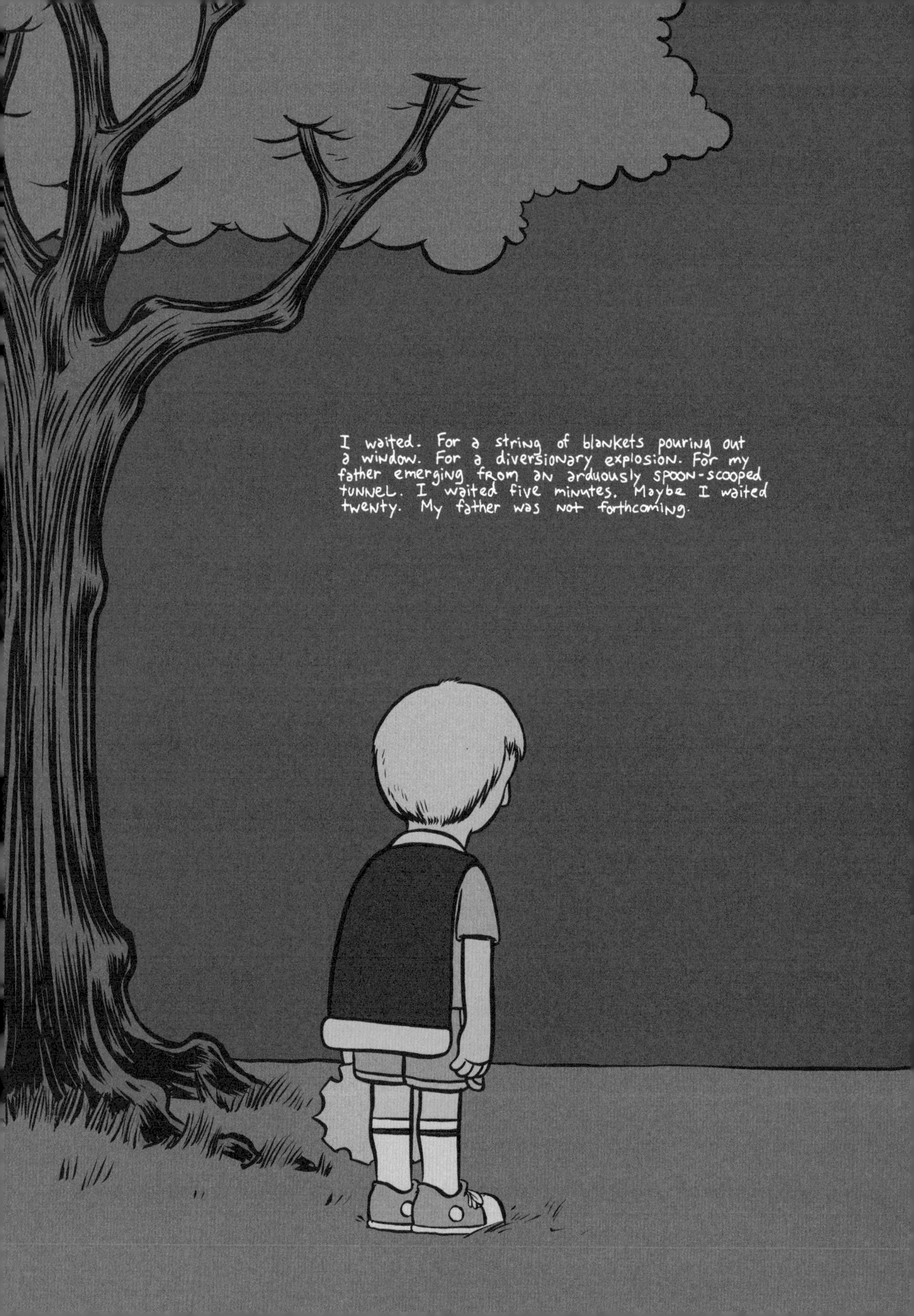
I waited. For a string of blankets pouring out a window. For a diversionary explosion. For my father emerging from an arduously spoon-scooped tunnel. I waited five minutes. Maybe I waited twenty. My father was not forthcoming.

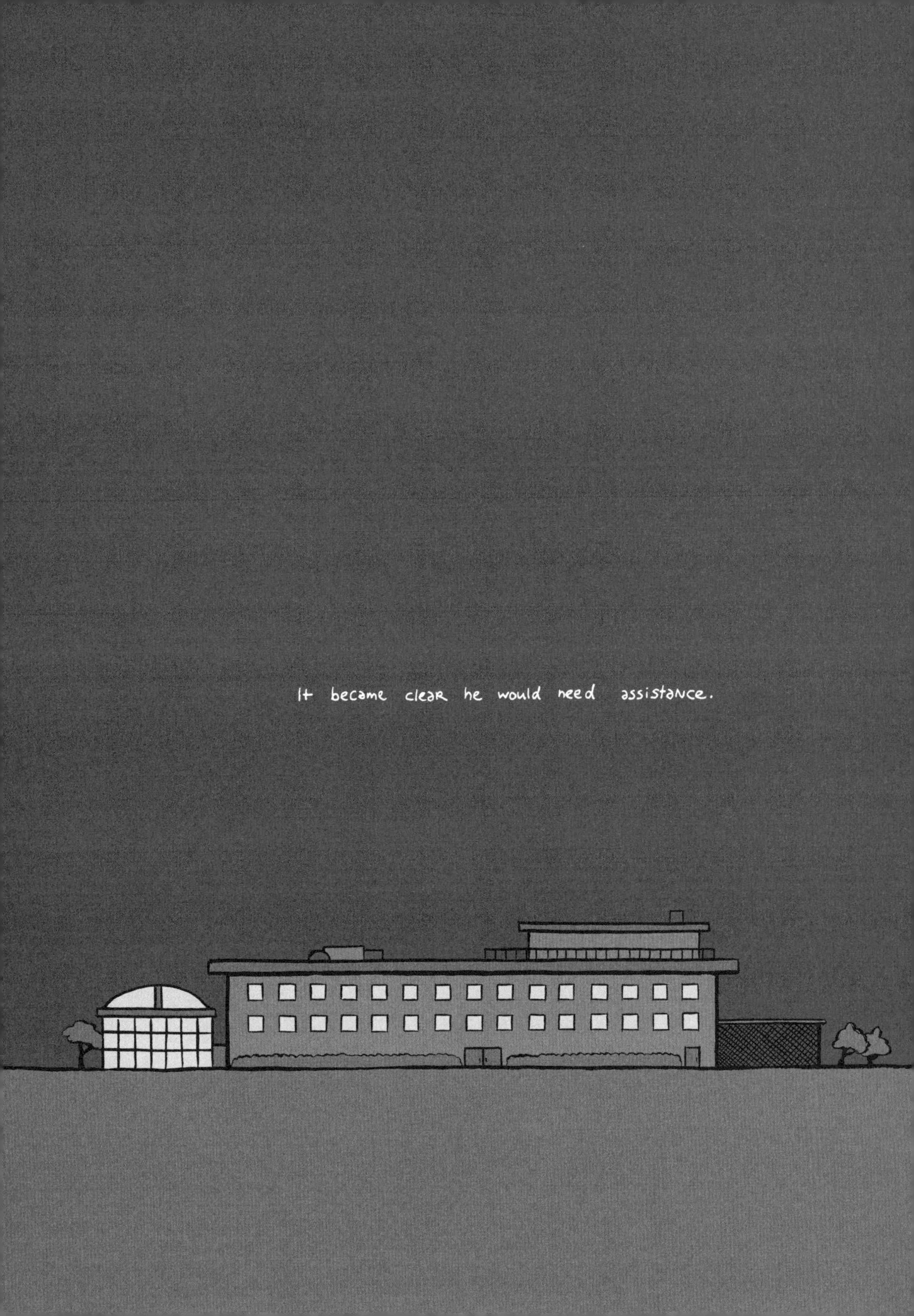
It became clear he would need assistance.

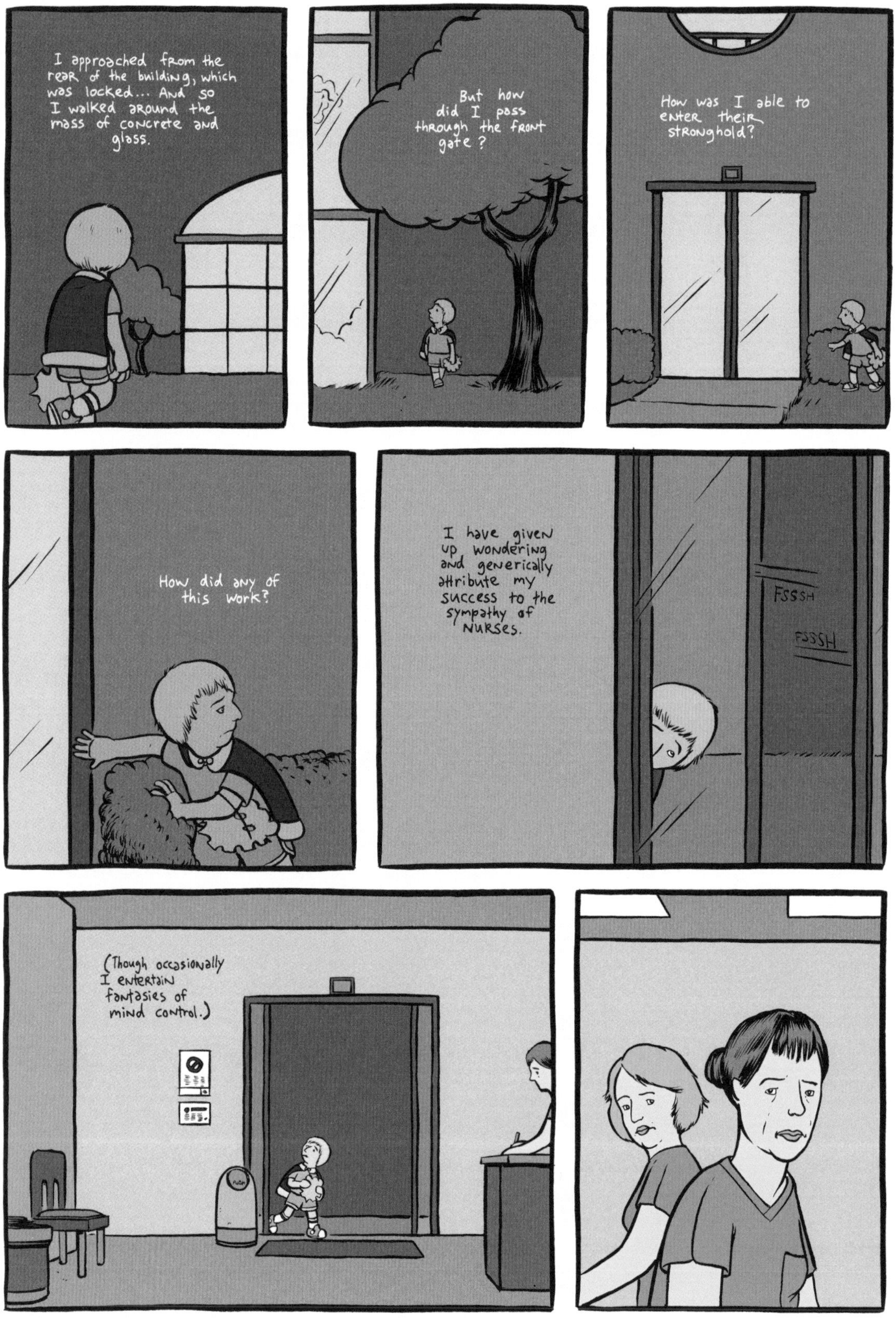

I approached from the rear of the building, which was locked... And so I walked around the mass of concrete and glass.
But how did I pass through the front gate?
How was I able to enter their stronghold?
How did any of this work?
I have given up wondering and generically attribute my success to the sympathy of nurses.
FSSSH
FSSSH
(Though occasionally I entertain fantasies of mind control.)

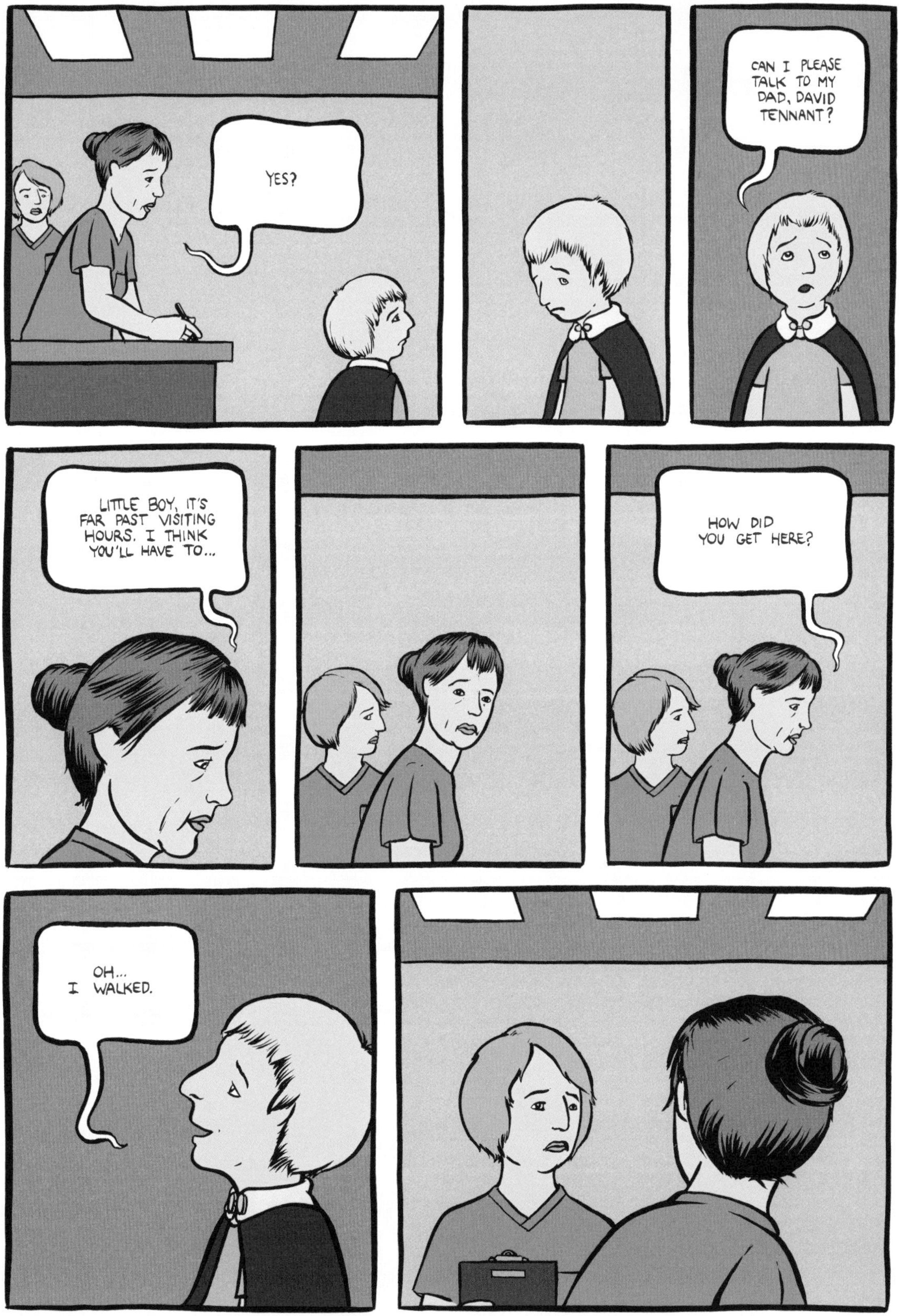
YES?
CAN I PLEASE TALK TO MY DAD, DAVID TENNANT?
LITTLE BOY, IT'S FAR PAST VISITING HOURS. I THINK YOU'LL HAVE TO...
HOW DID YOU GET HERE?
OH... I WALKED.

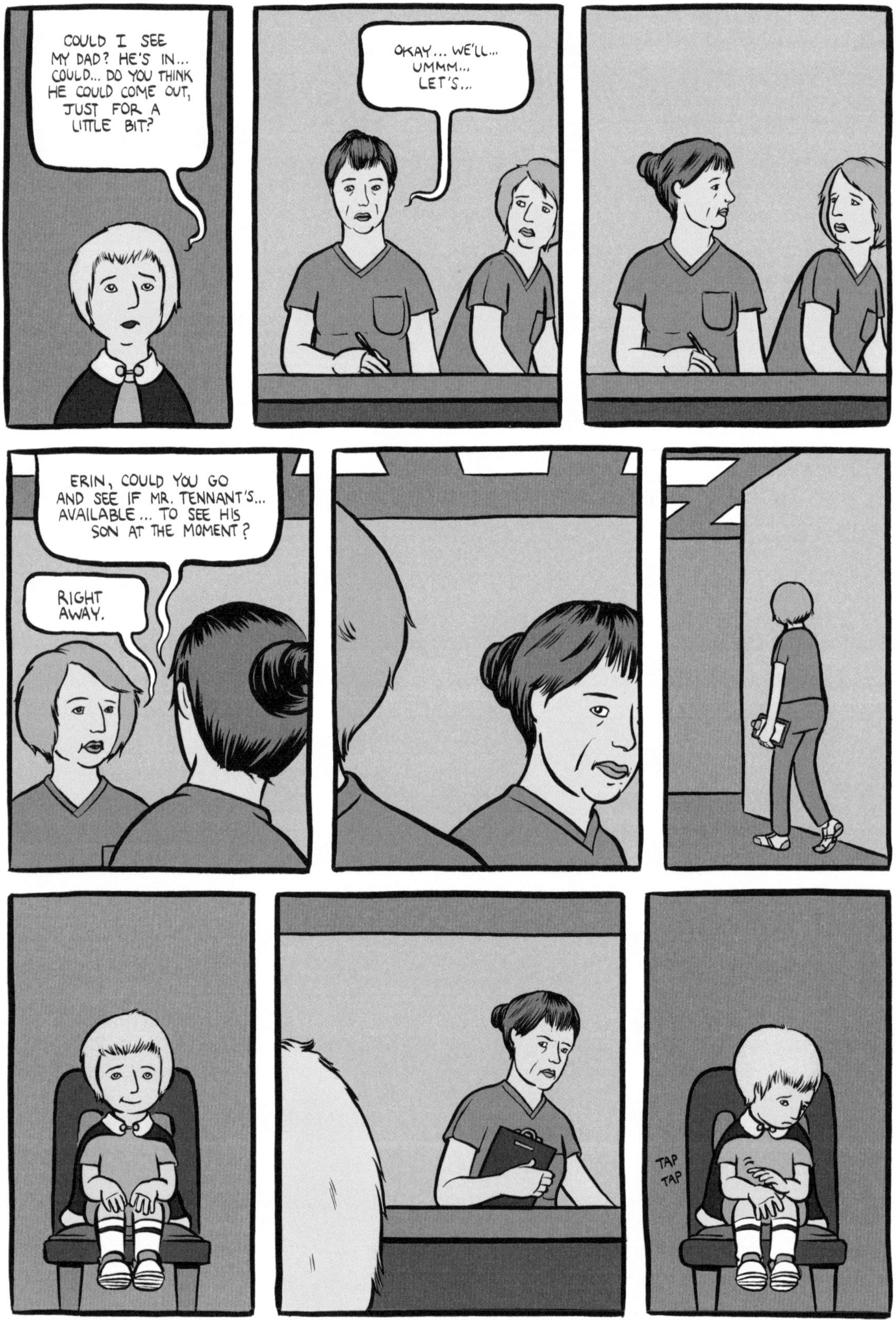
COULD I SEE MY DAD? HE'S IN... COULD... DO YOU THINK HE COULD COME OUT, JUST FOR A LITTLE BIT?
OKAY... WE'LL... UMMM... LET'S...
ERIN, COULD YOU GO AND SEE IF MR. TENNANT'S... AVAILABLE... TO SEE HIS SON AT THE MOMENT?
RIGHT AWAY.
TAP TAP

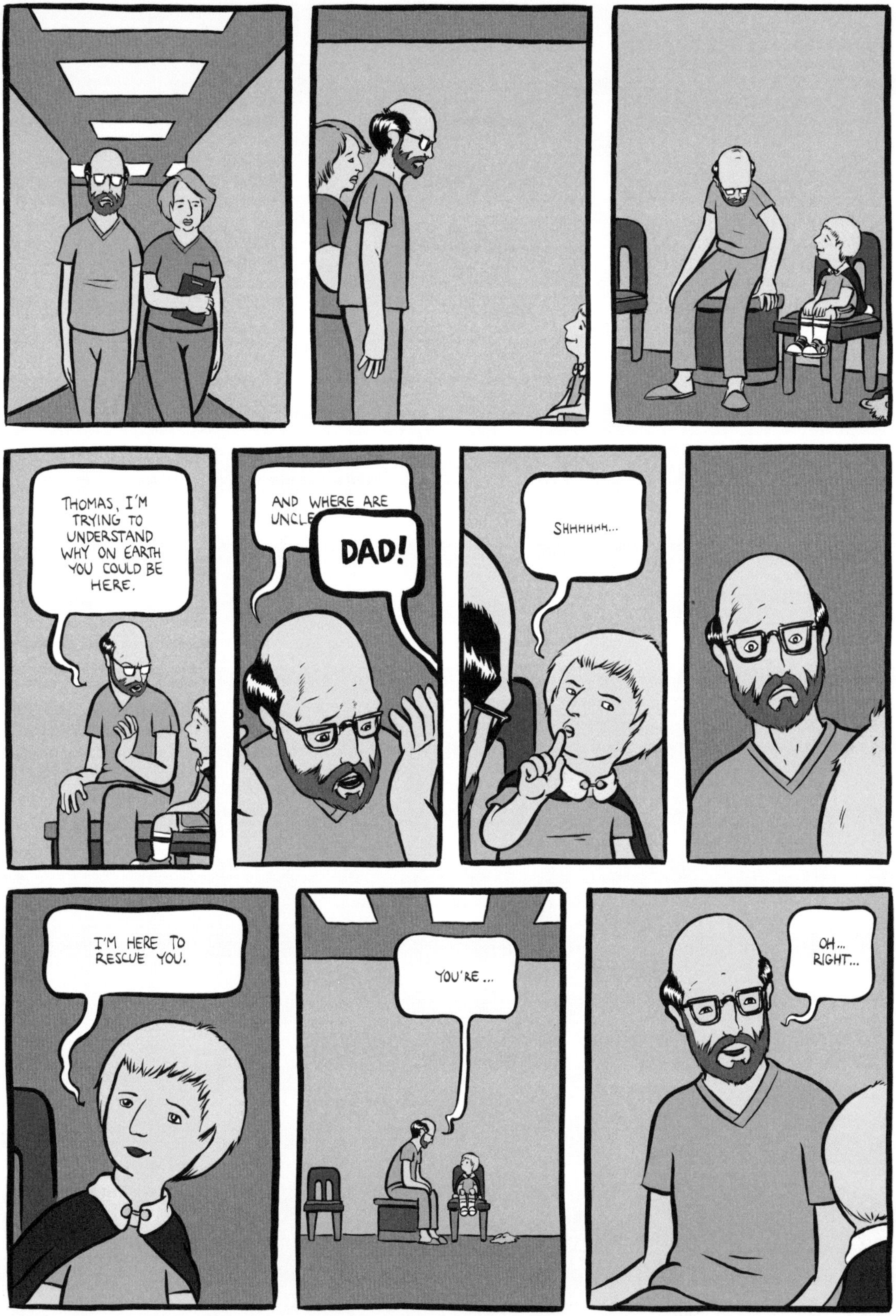
THOMAS, I'M TRYING TO UNDERSTAND WHY ON EARTH YOU COULD BE HERE.
AND WHERE ARE UNCLE
DAD!
SHHHHHH...
I'M HERE TO RESCUE YOU.
YOU'RE...
OH... RIGHT...

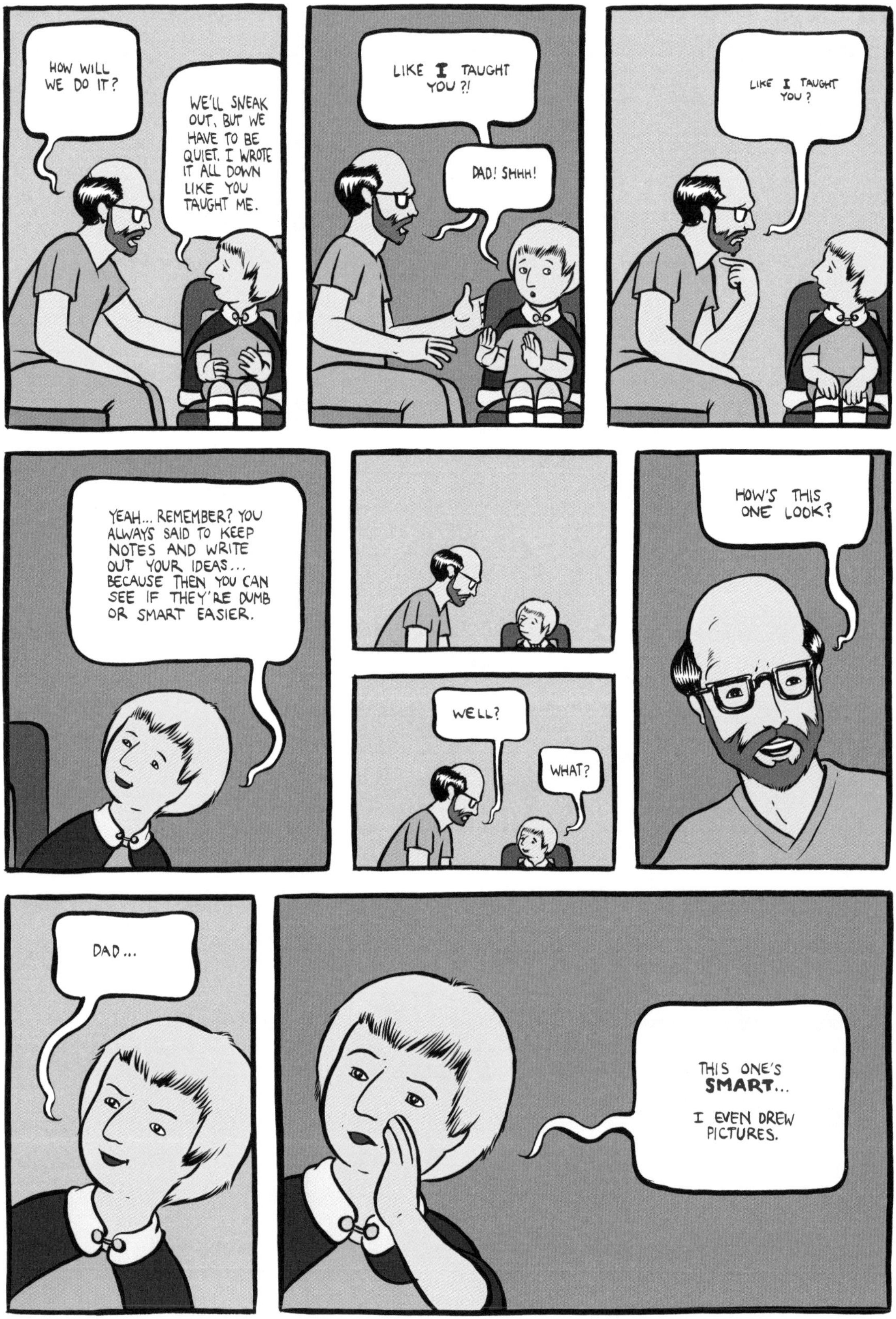
HOW WILL WE DO IT?
WE'LL SNEAK OUT, BUT WE HAVE TO BE QUIET. I WROTE IT ALL DOWN LIKE YOU TAUGHT ME.
LIKE **I** TAUGHT YOU ?!
DAD! SHHH!
LIKE **I** TAUGHT YOU ?
YEAH... REMEMBER? YOU ALWAYS SAID TO KEEP NOTES AND WRITE OUT YOUR IDEAS... BECAUSE THEN YOU CAN SEE IF THEY'RE DUMB OR SMART EASIER.
WELL?
WHAT?
HOW'S THIS ONE LOOK?
DAD...
THIS ONE'S **SMART**...
I EVEN DREW PICTURES.

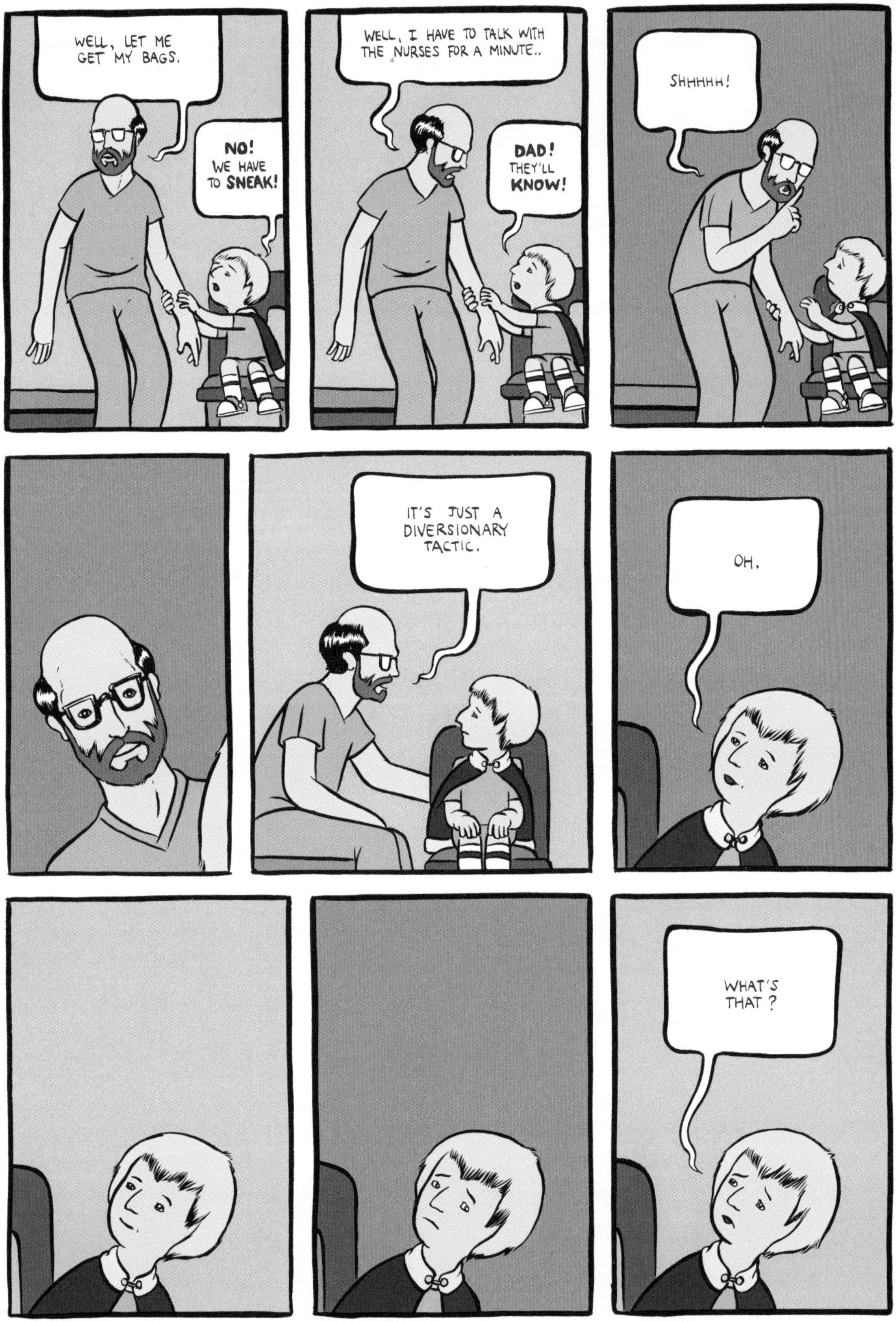
WELL, LET ME GET MY BAGS.
NO! WE HAVE TO SNEAK!
WELL, I HAVE TO TALK WITH THE NURSES FOR A MINUTE..
DAD! THEY'LL KNOW!
SHHHHH!
IT'S JUST A DIVERSIONARY TACTIC.
OH.
WHAT'S THAT?

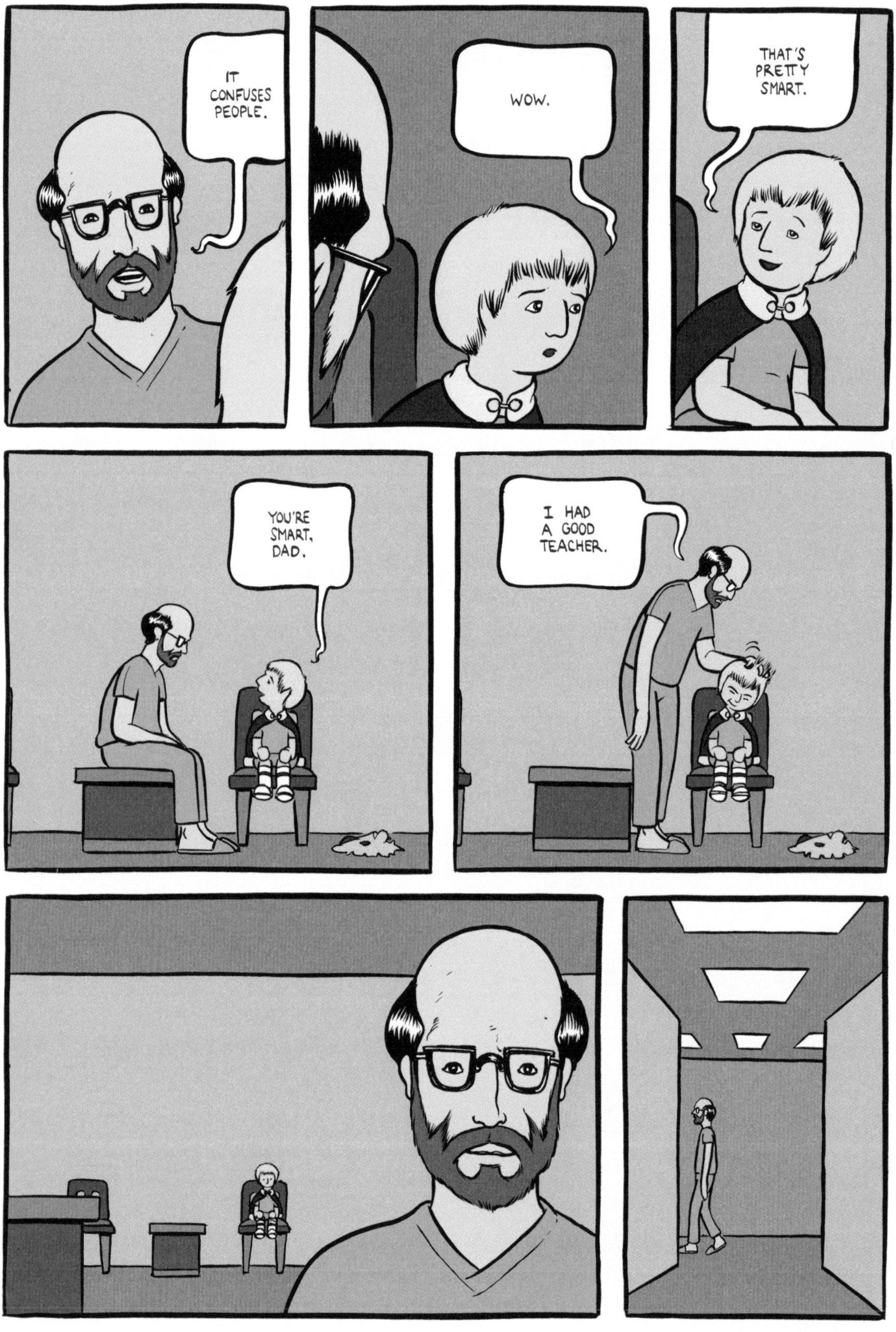
IT CONFUSES PEOPLE.
WOW.
THAT'S PRETTY SMART.
YOU'RE SMART, DAD.
I HAD A GOOD TEACHER.

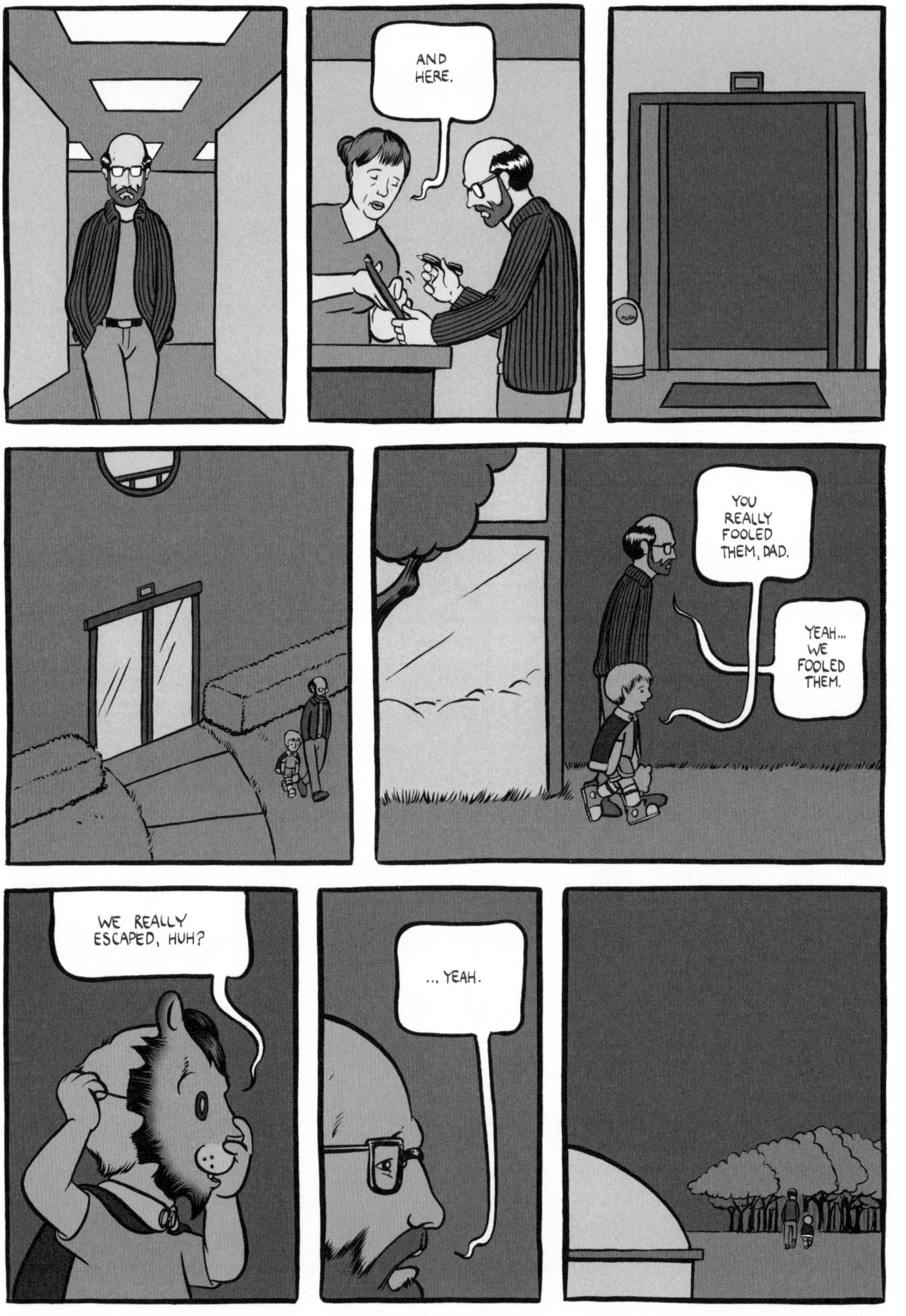
AND HERE.
YOU REALLY FOOLED THEM, DAD.
YEAH... WE FOOLED THEM.
WE REALLY ESCAPED, HUH?
... YEAH.

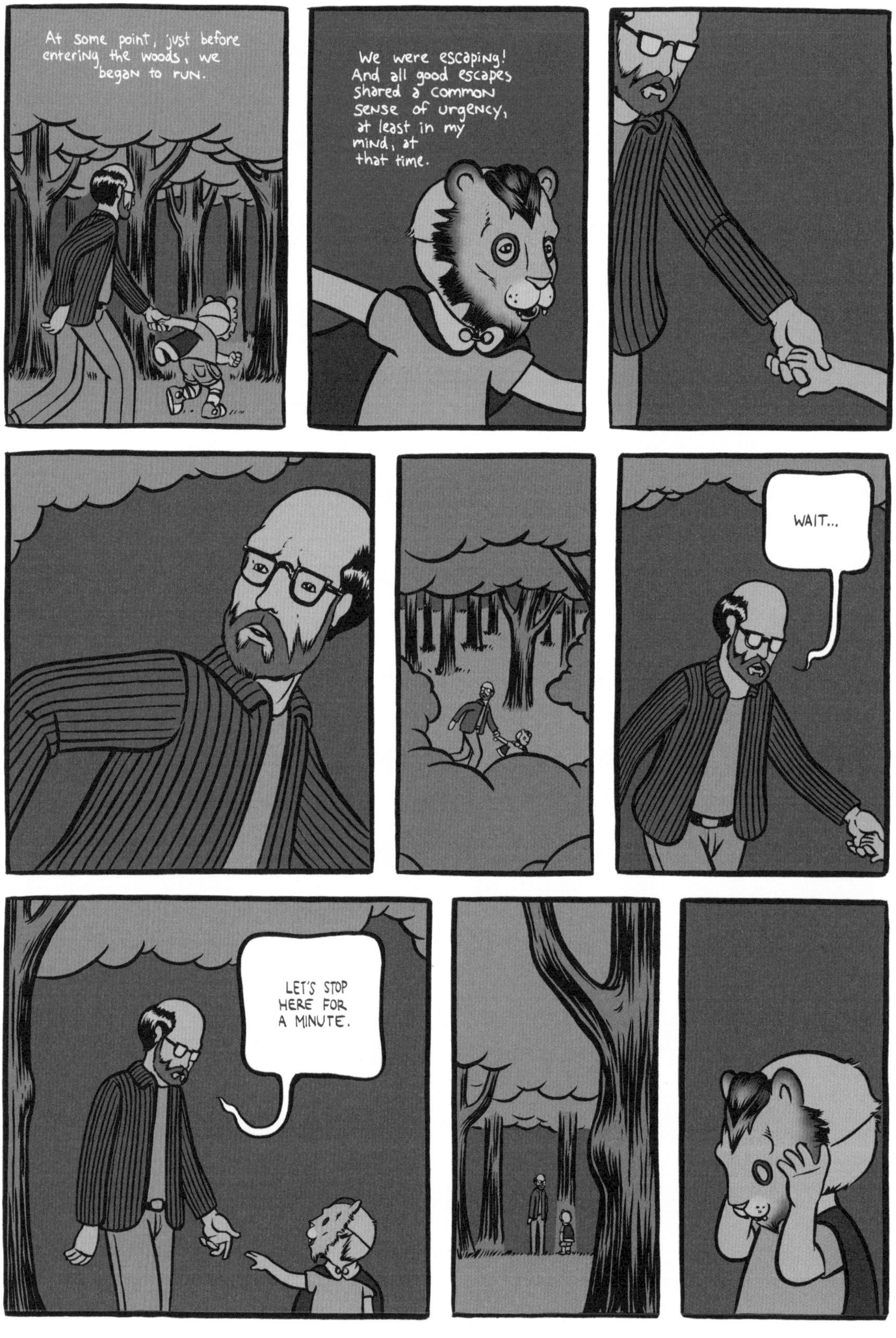
At some point, just before entering the woods, we began to run.
We were escaping! And all good escapes shared a common sense of urgency, at least in my mind, at that time.
WAIT...
LET'S STOP HERE FOR A MINUTE.

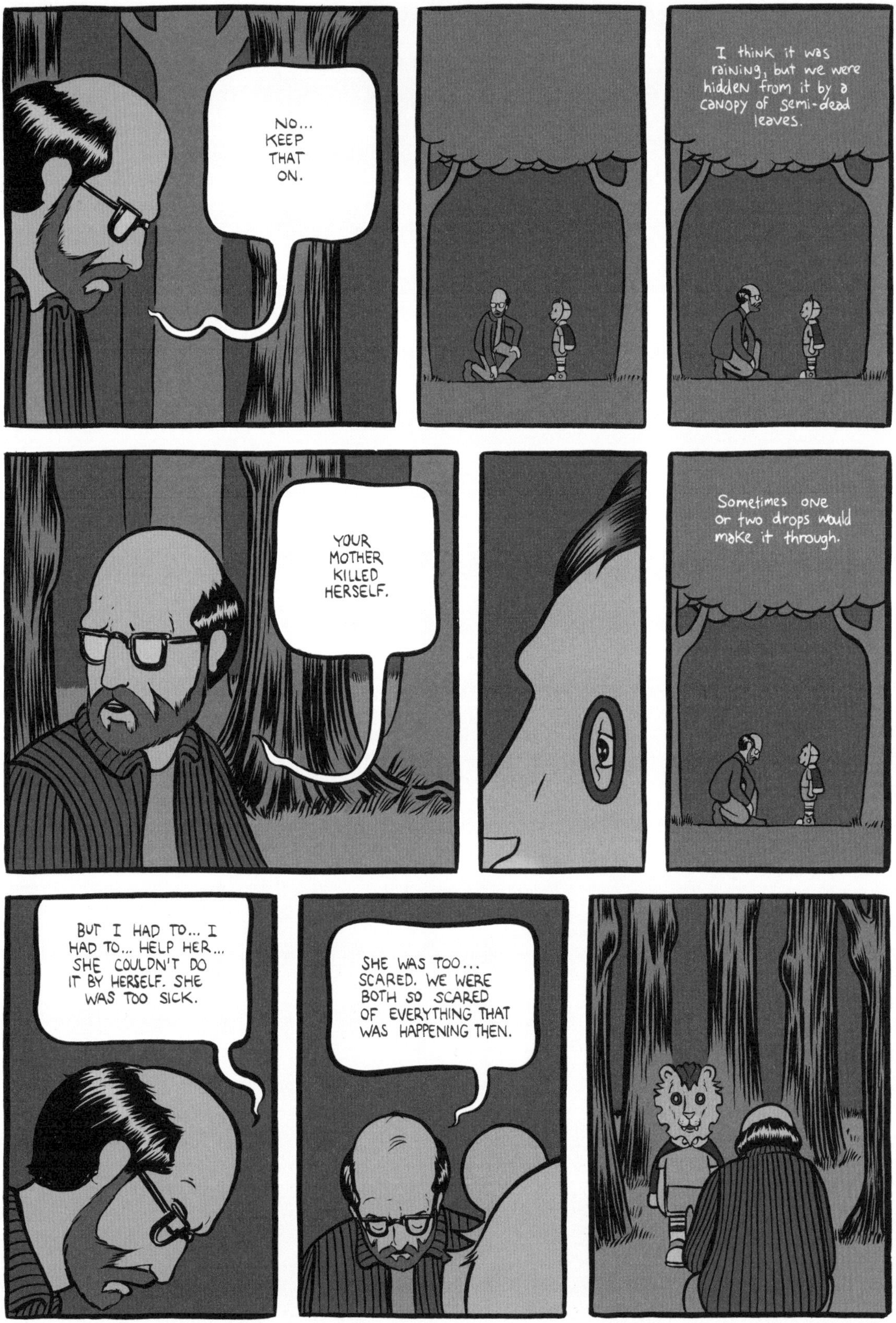
NO... KEEP THAT ON.
I think it was raining, but we were hidden from it by a canopy of semi-dead leaves.
YOUR MOTHER KILLED HERSELF.
Sometimes one or two drops would make it through.
BUT I HAD TO... I HAD TO... HELP HER... SHE COULDN'T DO IT BY HERSELF. SHE WAS TOO SICK.
SHE WAS TOO... SCARED. WE WERE BOTH SO SCARED OF EVERYTHING THAT WAS HAPPENING THEN.

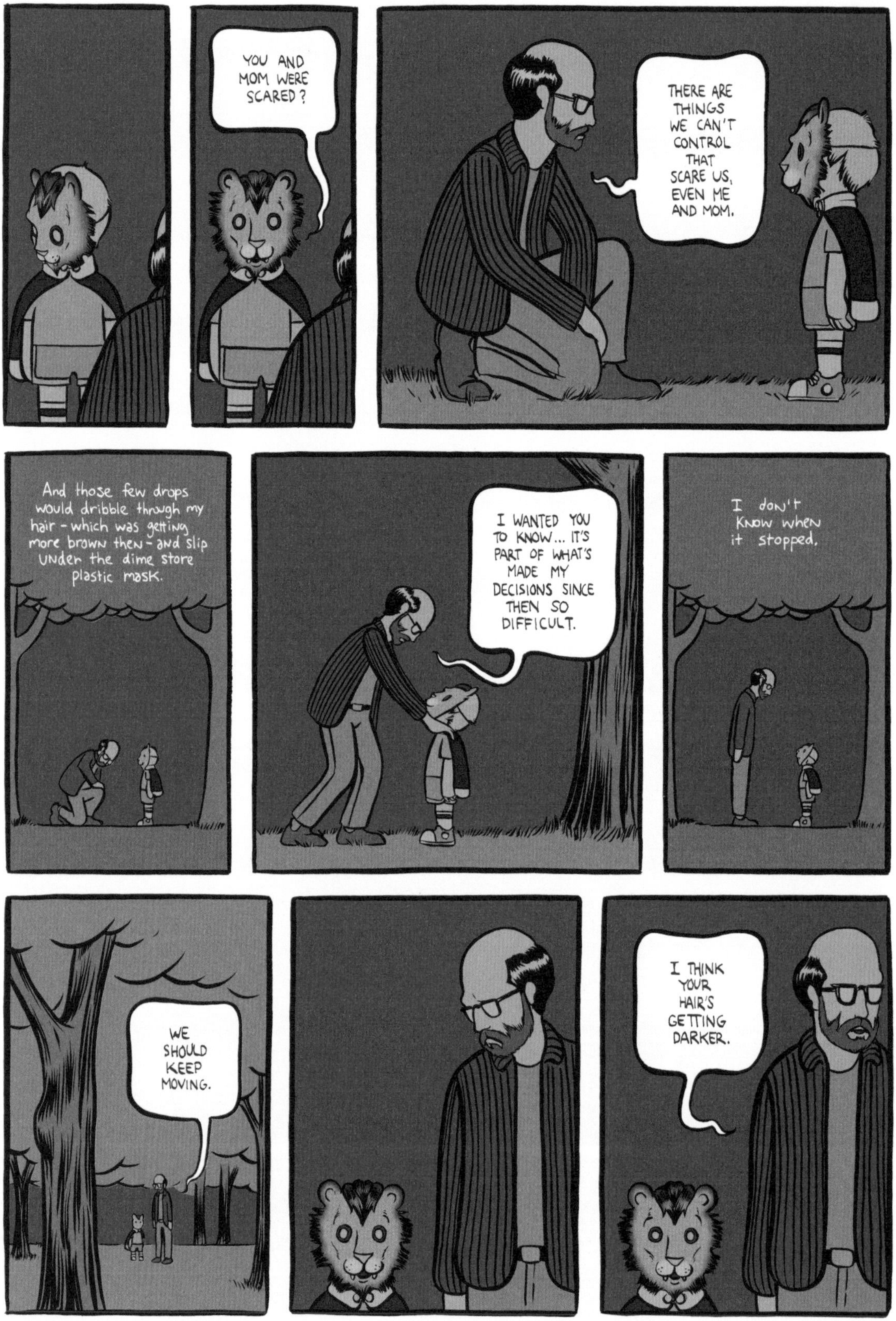
YOU AND MOM WERE SCARED?
THERE ARE THINGS WE CAN'T CONTROL THAT SCARE US, EVEN ME AND MOM.
And those few drops would dribble through my hair - which was getting more brown then - and slip under the dime store plastic mask.
I WANTED YOU TO KNOW... IT'S PART OF WHAT'S MADE MY DECISIONS SINCE THEN SO DIFFICULT.
I don't know when it stopped.
WE SHOULD KEEP MOVING.
I THINK YOUR HAIR'S GETTING DARKER.

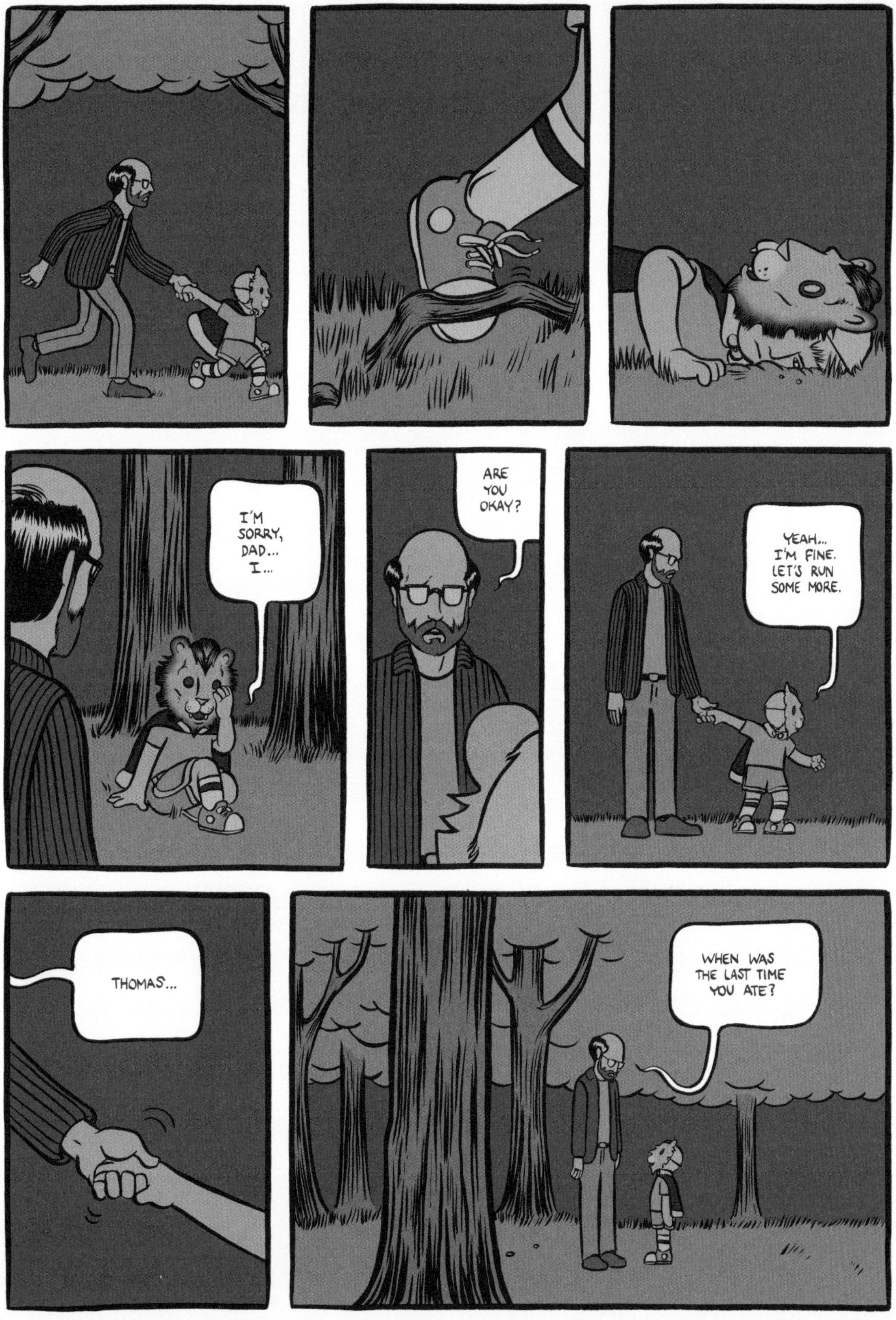
I'M SORRY, DAD... I...
ARE YOU OKAY?
YEAH... I'M FINE. LET'S RUN SOME MORE.
THOMAS...
WHEN WAS THE LAST TIME YOU ATE?

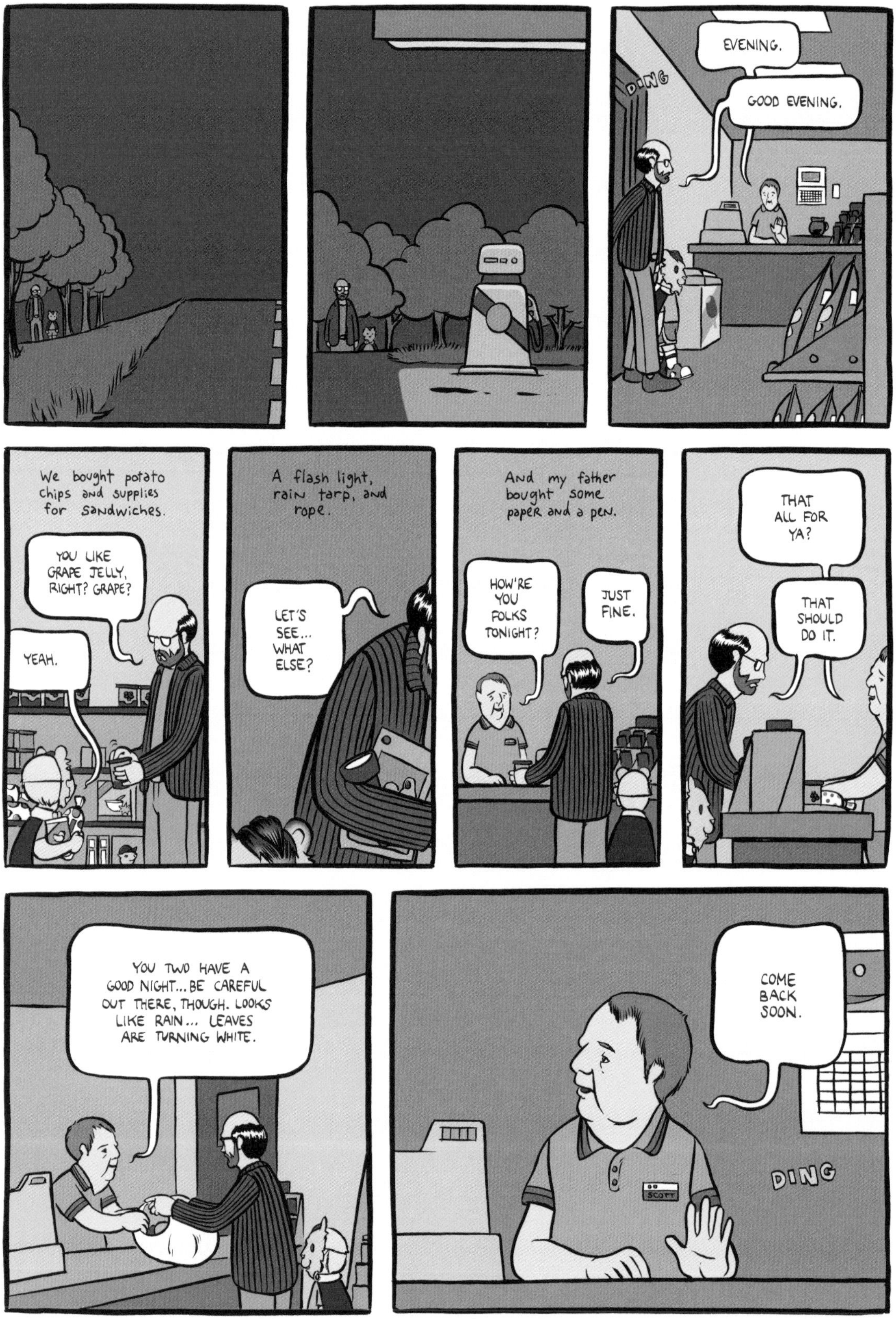
EVENING.
GOOD EVENING.
DING
We bought potato chips and supplies for sandwiches.
YOU LIKE GRAPE JELLY, RIGHT? GRAPE?
YEAH.
A flash light, rain tarp, and rope.
LET'S SEE... WHAT ELSE?
And my father bought some paper and a pen.
HOW'RE YOU FOLKS TONIGHT?
JUST FINE.
THAT ALL FOR YA?
THAT SHOULD DO IT.
YOU TWO HAVE A GOOD NIGHT... BE CAREFUL OUT THERE, THOUGH. LOOKS LIKE RAIN... LEAVES ARE TURNING WHITE.
COME BACK SOON.
SCOTT
DING

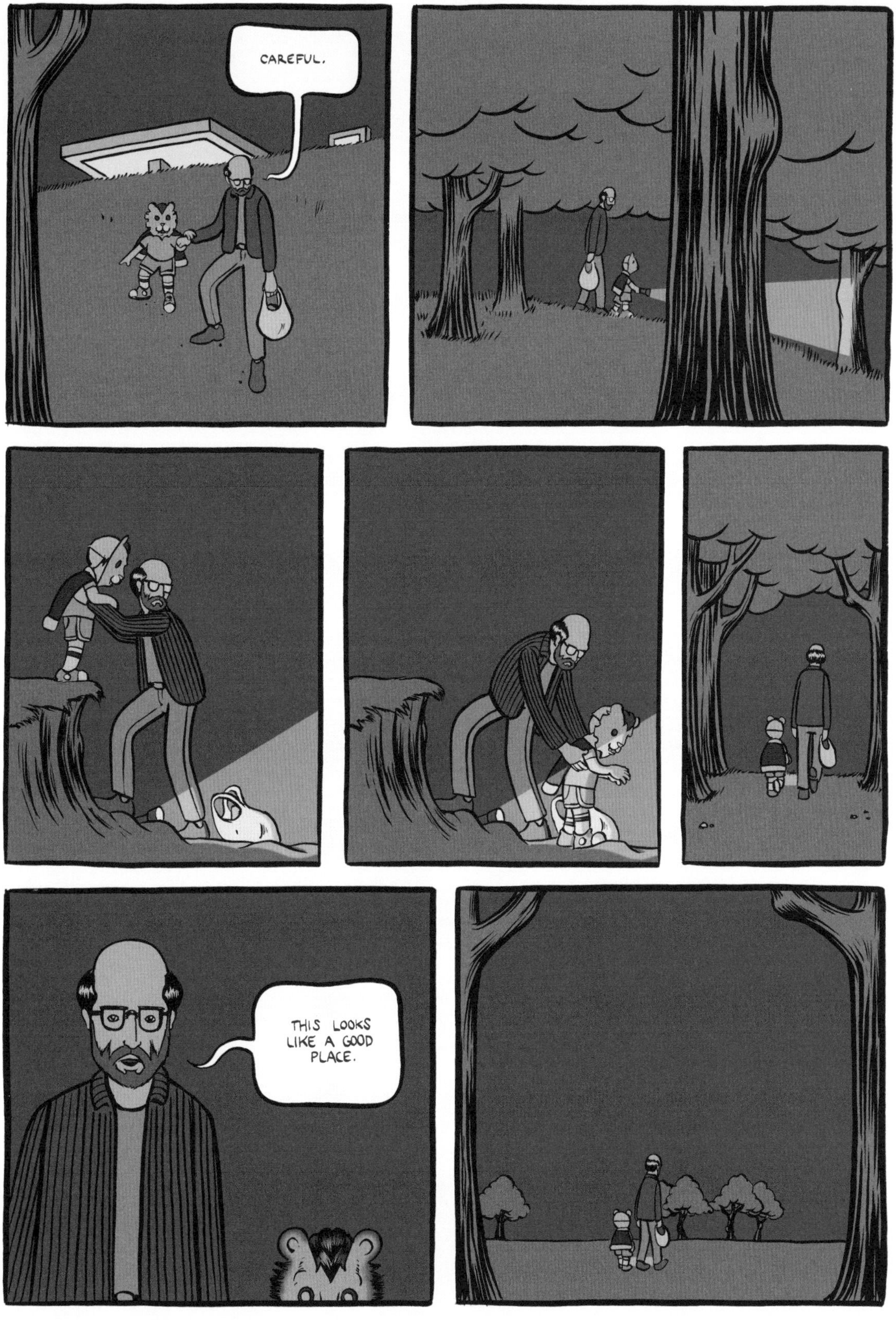
CAREFUL.
THIS LOOKS LIKE A GOOD PLACE.

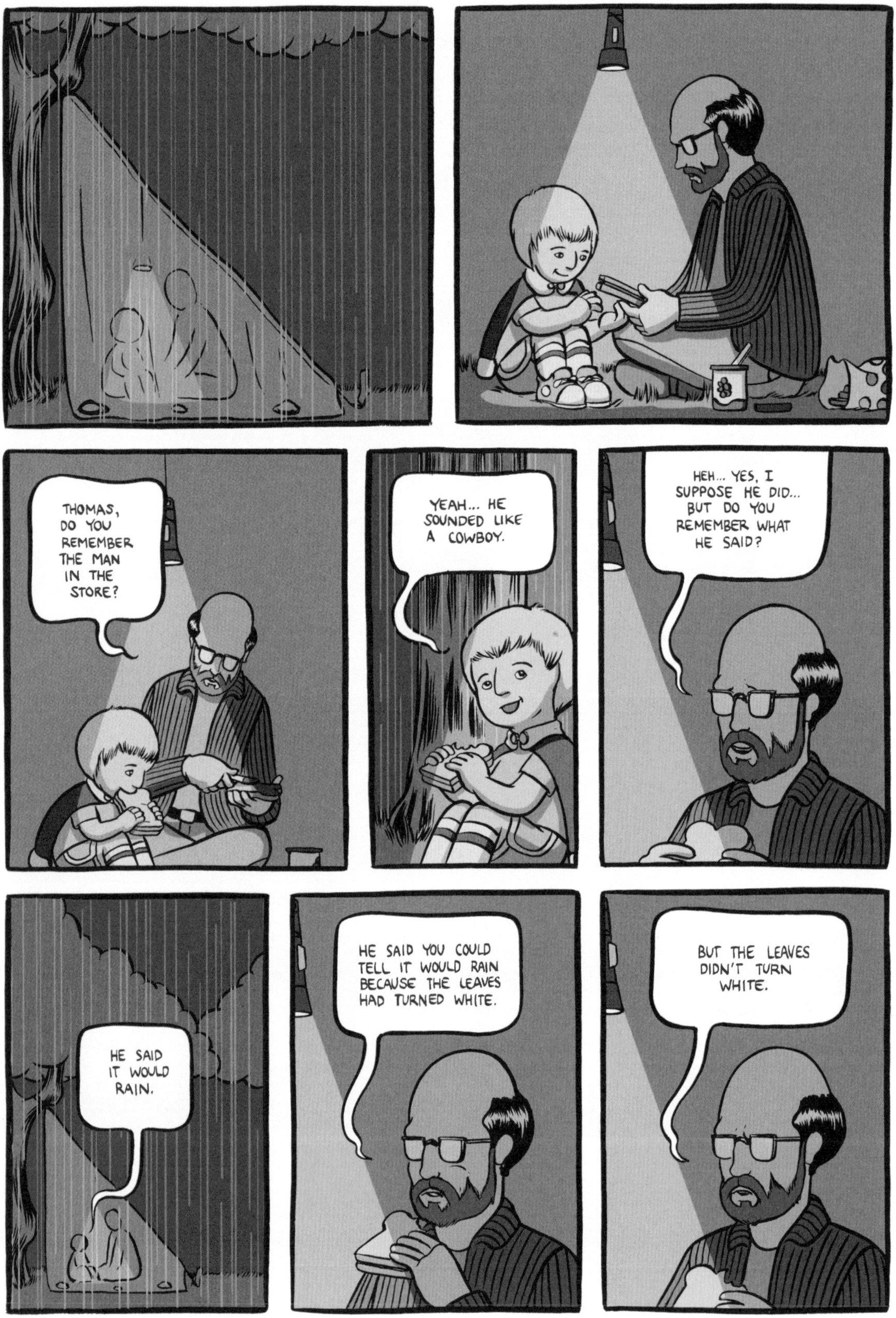
THOMAS, DO YOU REMEMBER THE MAN IN THE STORE?
YEAH... HE SOUNDED LIKE A COWBOY.
HEH... YES, I SUPPOSE HE DID... BUT DO YOU REMEMBER WHAT HE SAID?
HE SAID IT WOULD RAIN.
HE SAID YOU COULD TELL IT WOULD RAIN BECAUSE THE LEAVES HAD TURNED WHITE.
BUT THE LEAVES DIDN'T TURN WHITE.

"The leaves do not turn white," he said calmly.

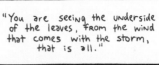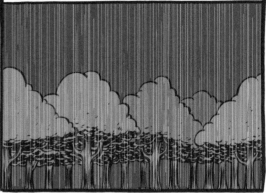
"You are seeing the underside of the leaves, from the wind that comes with the storm, that is all."

"People create... little systems of explanation."

"Things that are not really true, but are easier to digest than the intricacies of reality."

CLICK

LET'S TRY TO GET SOME SLEEP NOW.

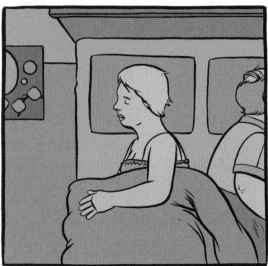

How unaware, or perhaps unaccepting, were we of the realities that had befallen us?

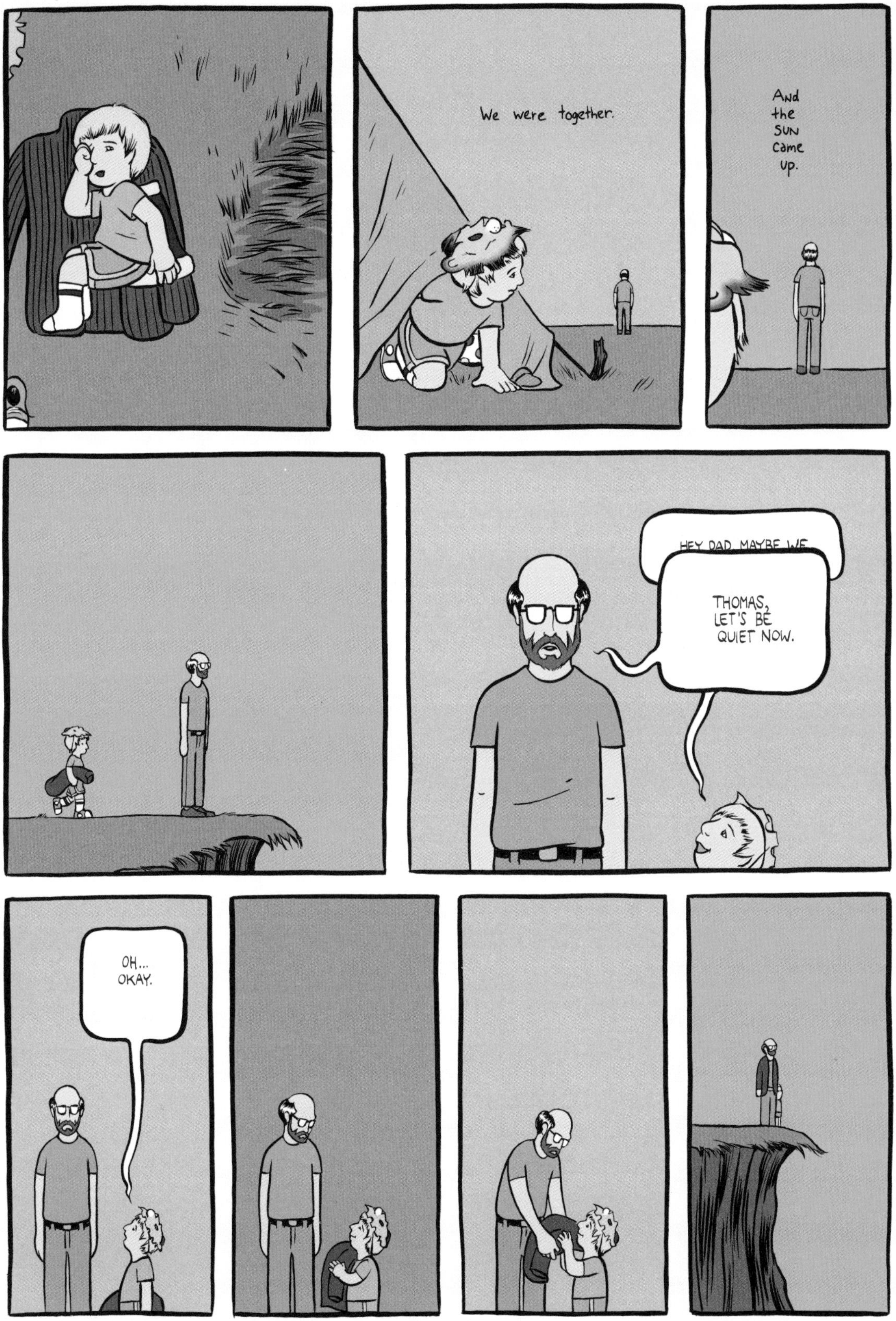
We were together.
And the SUN came up.
HEY DAD, MAYBE WE
THOMAS, LET'S BE QUIET NOW.
OH... OKAY.

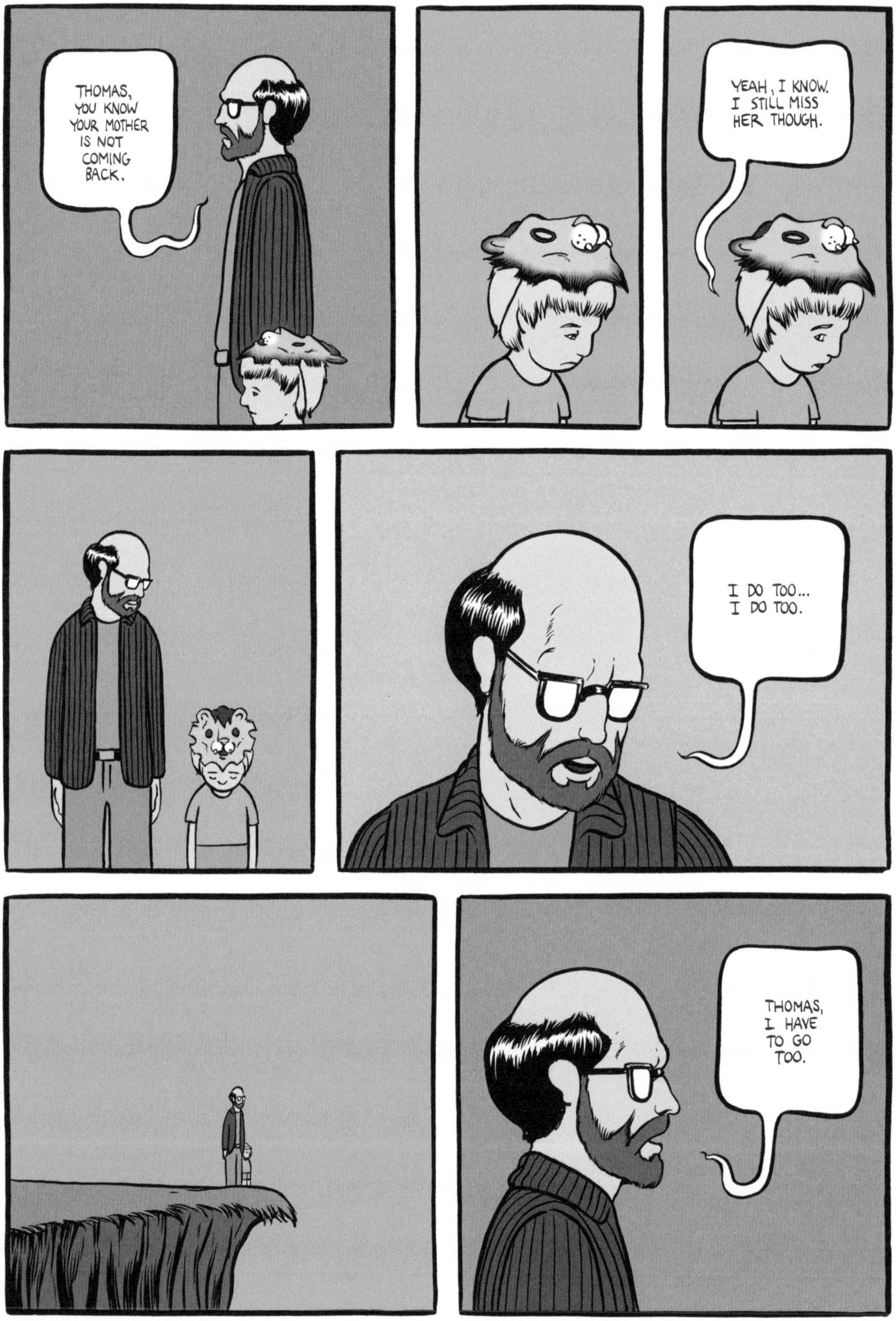
THOMAS, YOU KNOW YOUR MOTHER IS NOT COMING BACK.
YEAH, I KNOW. I STILL MISS HER THOUGH.
I DO TOO... I DO TOO.
THOMAS, I HAVE TO GO TOO.

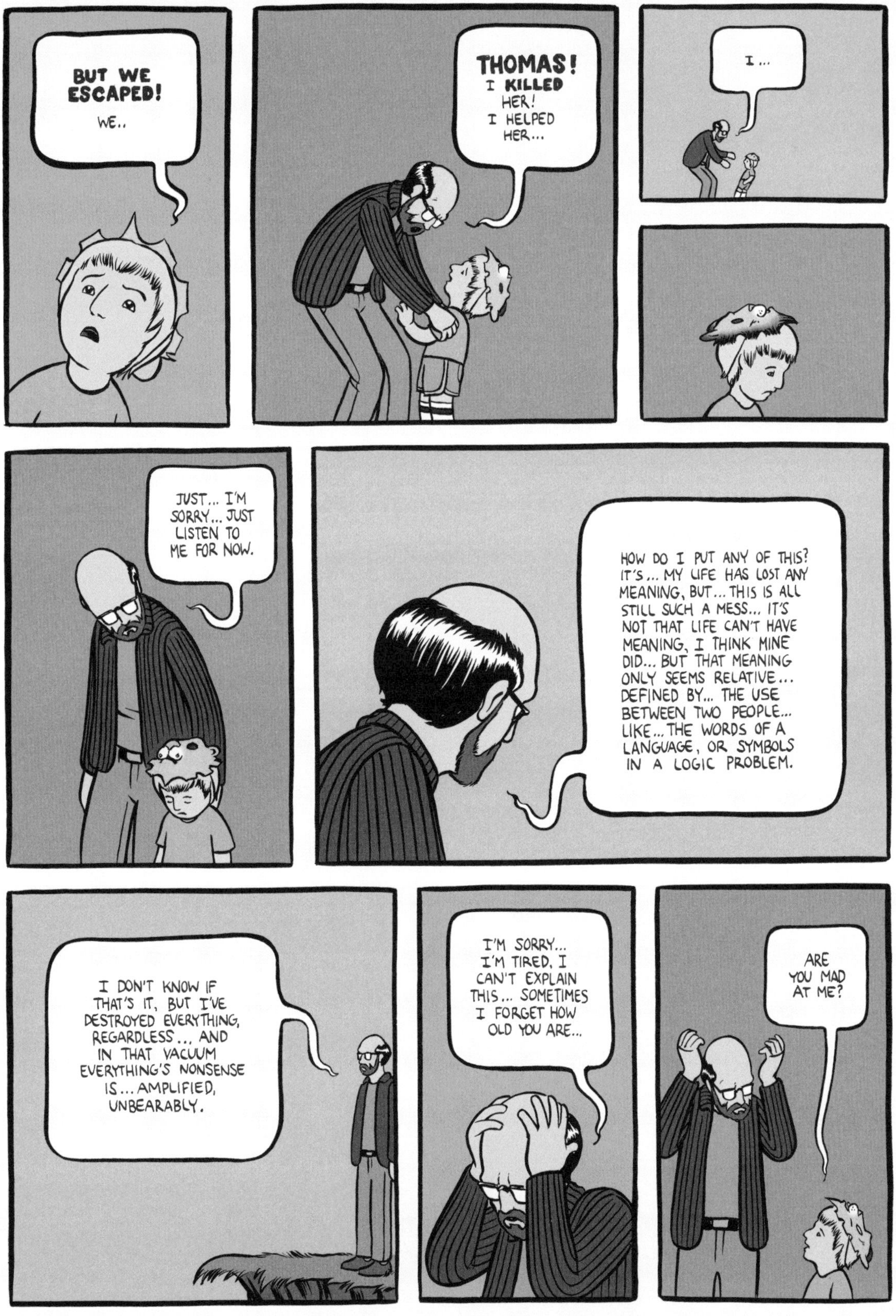

BUT WE ESCAPED! WE..
THOMAS! I KILLED HER! I HELPED HER...
I...
JUST... I'M SORRY... JUST LISTEN TO ME FOR NOW.
HOW DO I PUT ANY OF THIS? IT'S... MY LIFE HAS LOST ANY MEANING, BUT... THIS IS ALL STILL SUCH A MESS... IT'S NOT THAT LIFE CAN'T HAVE MEANING, I THINK MINE DID... BUT THAT MEANING ONLY SEEMS RELATIVE... DEFINED BY... THE USE BETWEEN TWO PEOPLE... LIKE... THE WORDS OF A LANGUAGE, OR SYMBOLS IN A LOGIC PROBLEM.
I DON'T KNOW IF THAT'S IT, BUT I'VE DESTROYED EVERYTHING, REGARDLESS..., AND IN THAT VACUUM EVERYTHING'S NONSENSE IS... AMPLIFIED, UNBEARABLY.
I'M SORRY... I'M TIRED, I CAN'T EXPLAIN THIS... SOMETIMES I FORGET HOW OLD YOU ARE...
ARE YOU MAD AT ME?

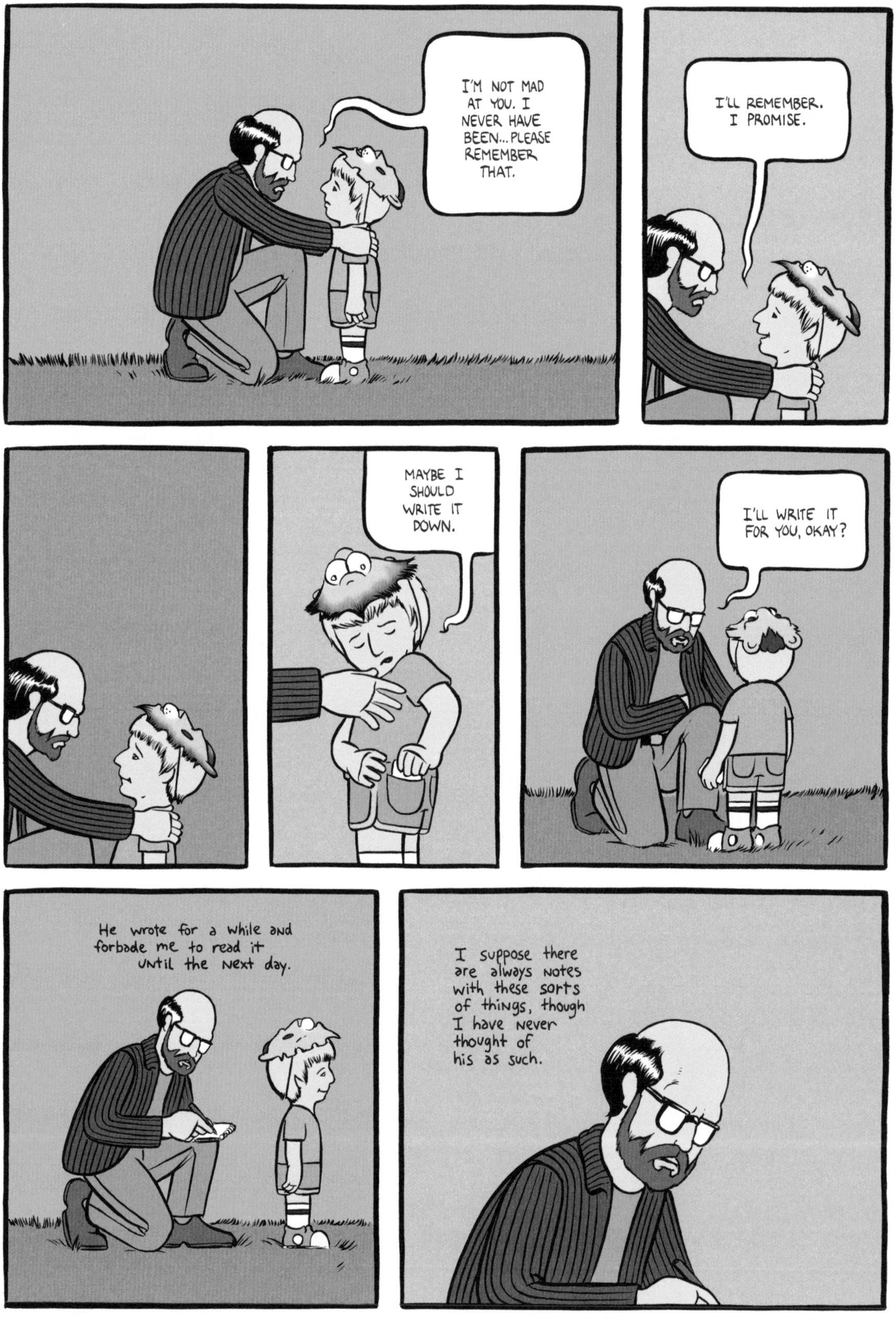
I'M NOT MAD AT YOU. I NEVER HAVE BEEN... PLEASE REMEMBER THAT.
I'LL REMEMBER. I PROMISE.
MAYBE I SHOULD WRITE IT DOWN.
I'LL WRITE IT FOR YOU, OKAY?
He wrote for a while and forbade me to read it until the next day.
I suppose there are always notes with these sorts of things, though I have never thought of his as such.

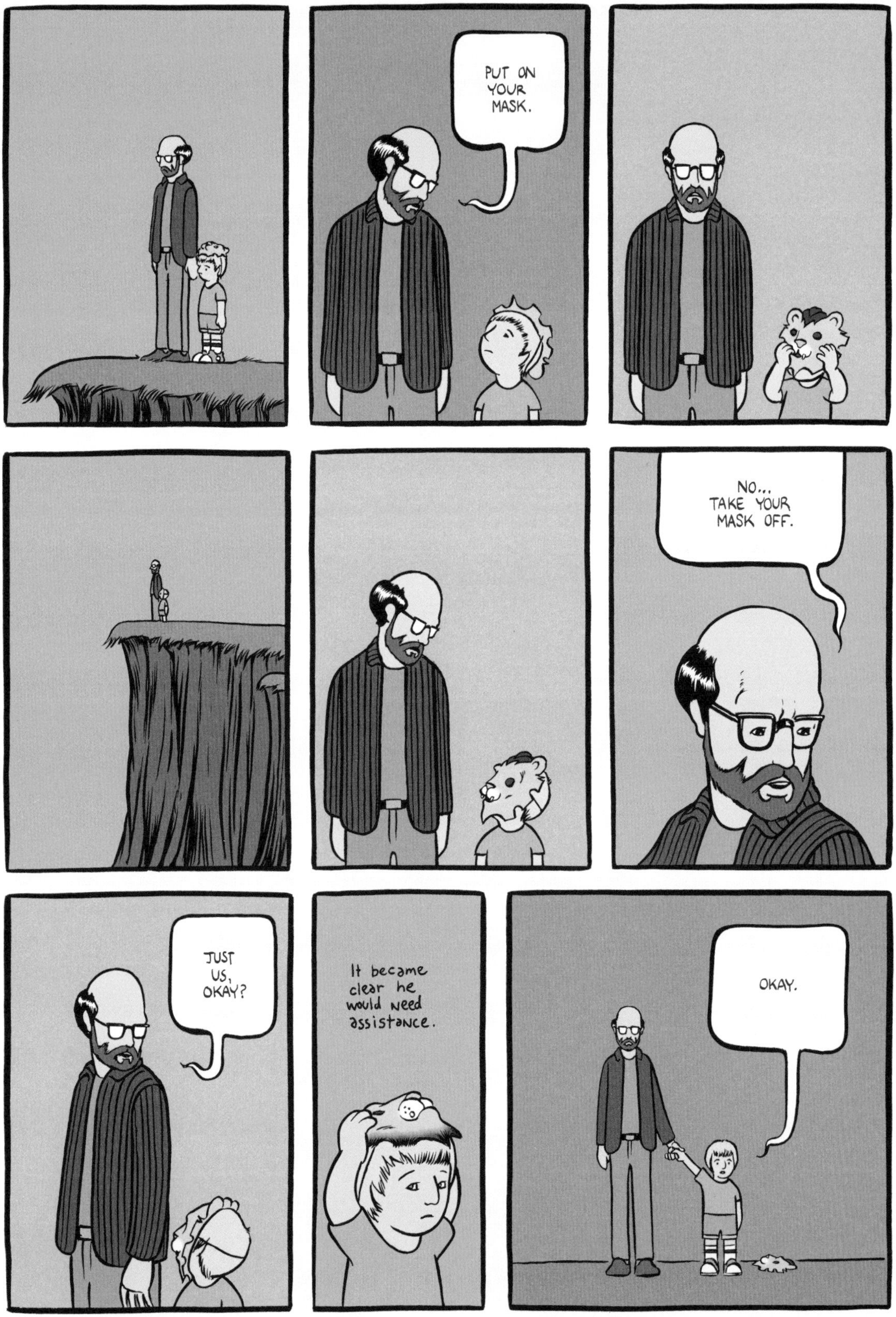
PUT ON YOUR MASK.
NO... TAKE YOUR MASK OFF.
JUST US, OKAY?
It became clear he would need assistance.
OKAY.

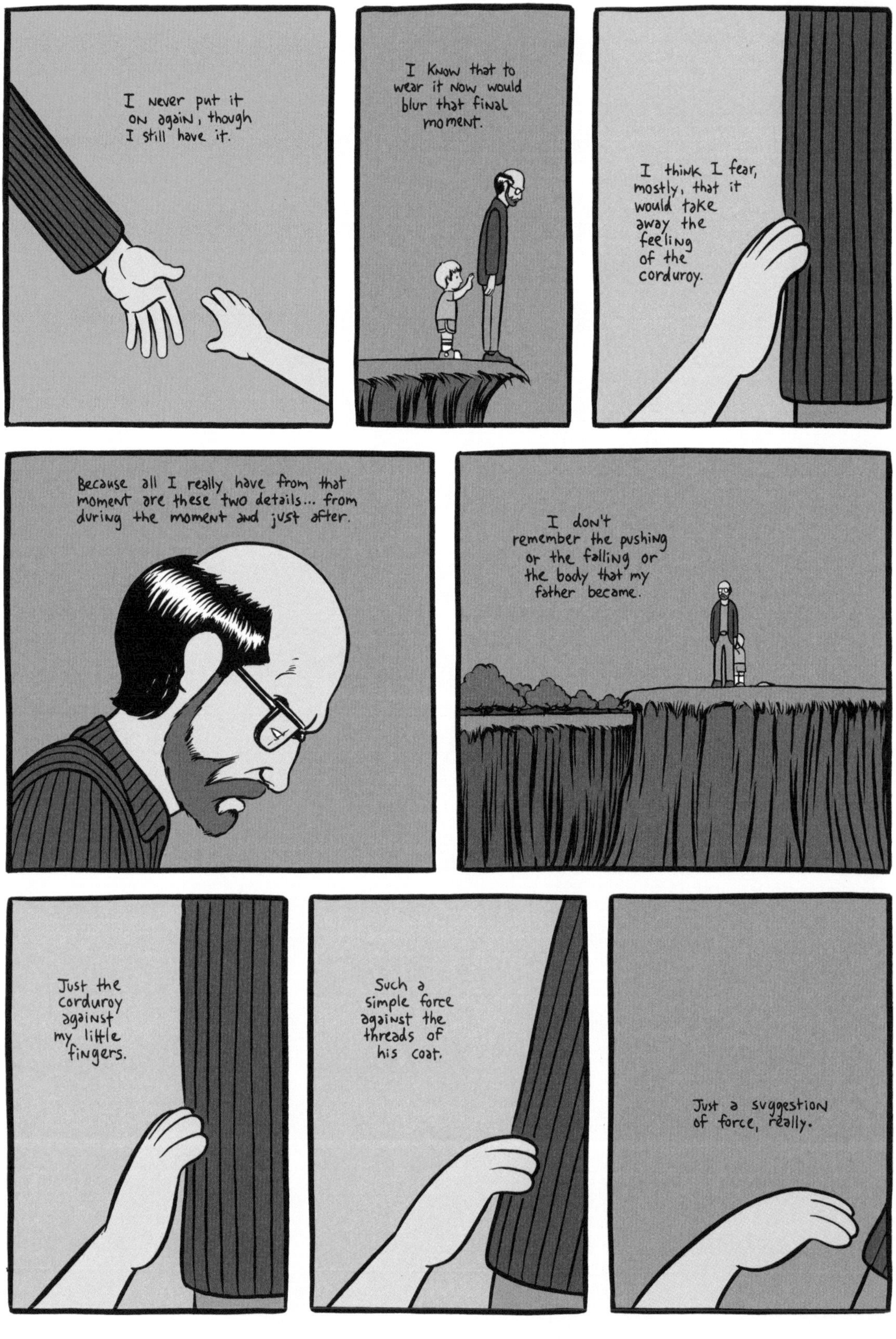
I never put it on again, though I still have it.
I know that to wear it now would blur that final moment.
I think I fear, mostly, that it would take away the feeling of the corduroy.
Because all I really have from that moment are these two details... from during the moment and just after.
I don't remember the pushing or the falling or the body that my father became.
Just the corduroy against my little fingers.
Such a simple force against the threads of his coat.
Just a suggestion of force, really.

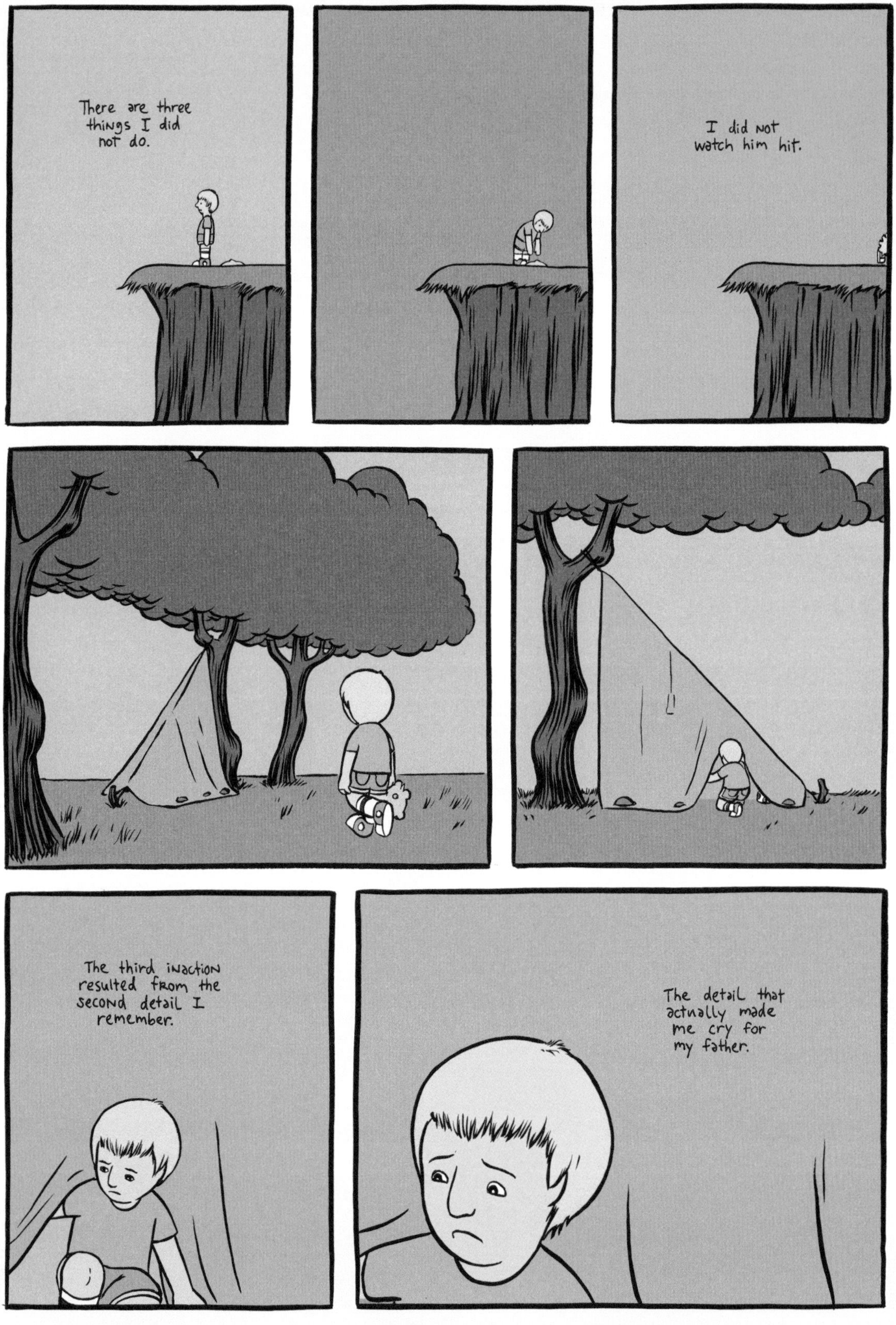
There are three things I did not do.
I did not watch him hit.
The third inaction resulted from the second detail I remember.
The detail that actually made me cry for my father.

His sandwich.

Of which
he had eaten
only three or
four bites.

Somehow this
forced him deeper
onto those stones.

This made his
ribcage cut through
his skin.

This stained his coat
in the patterns of the
jelly that breached the
paper hide of that
bread.

I sat and held it
for the longest time
I have ever
experienced.

The third inaction
was not eating
the sandwich.

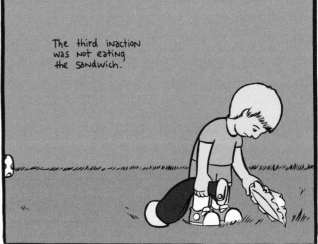

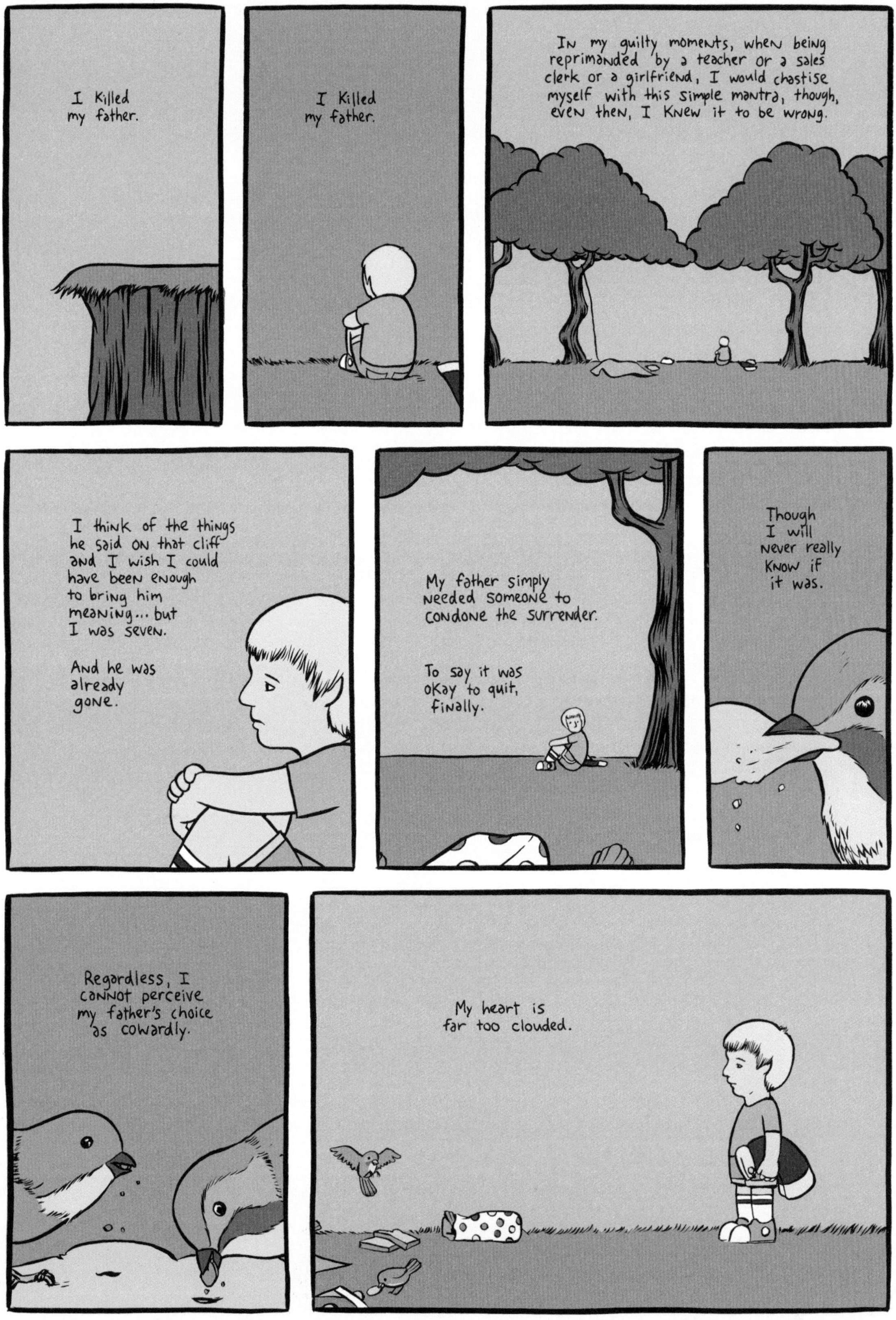

I Killed my father.
I Killed my father.
In my guilty moments, when being reprimanded by a teacher or a sales clerk or a girlfriend, I would chastise myself with this simple mantra, though, even then, I Knew it to be wrong.
I think of the things he said on that cliff and I wish I could have been enough to bring him meaning... but I was seven.
And he was already gone.
My father simply needed someone to condone the surrender.
To say it was okay to quit, finally.
Though I will never really Know if it was.
Regardless, I cannot perceive my father's choice as cowardly.
My heart is far too clouded.

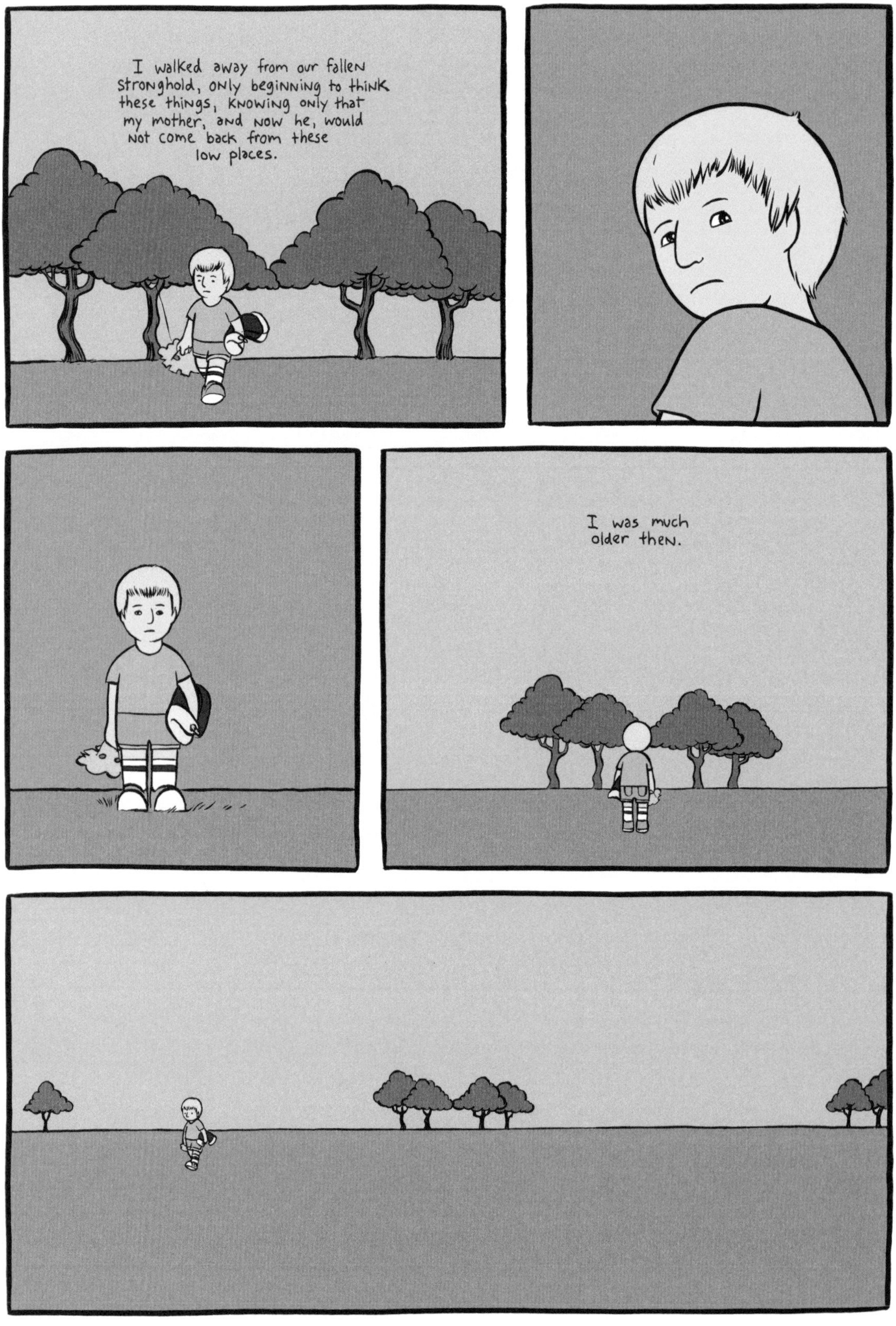
I walked away from our fallen stronghold, only beginning to think these things, knowing only that my mother, and now he, would not come back from these low places.
I was much older then.

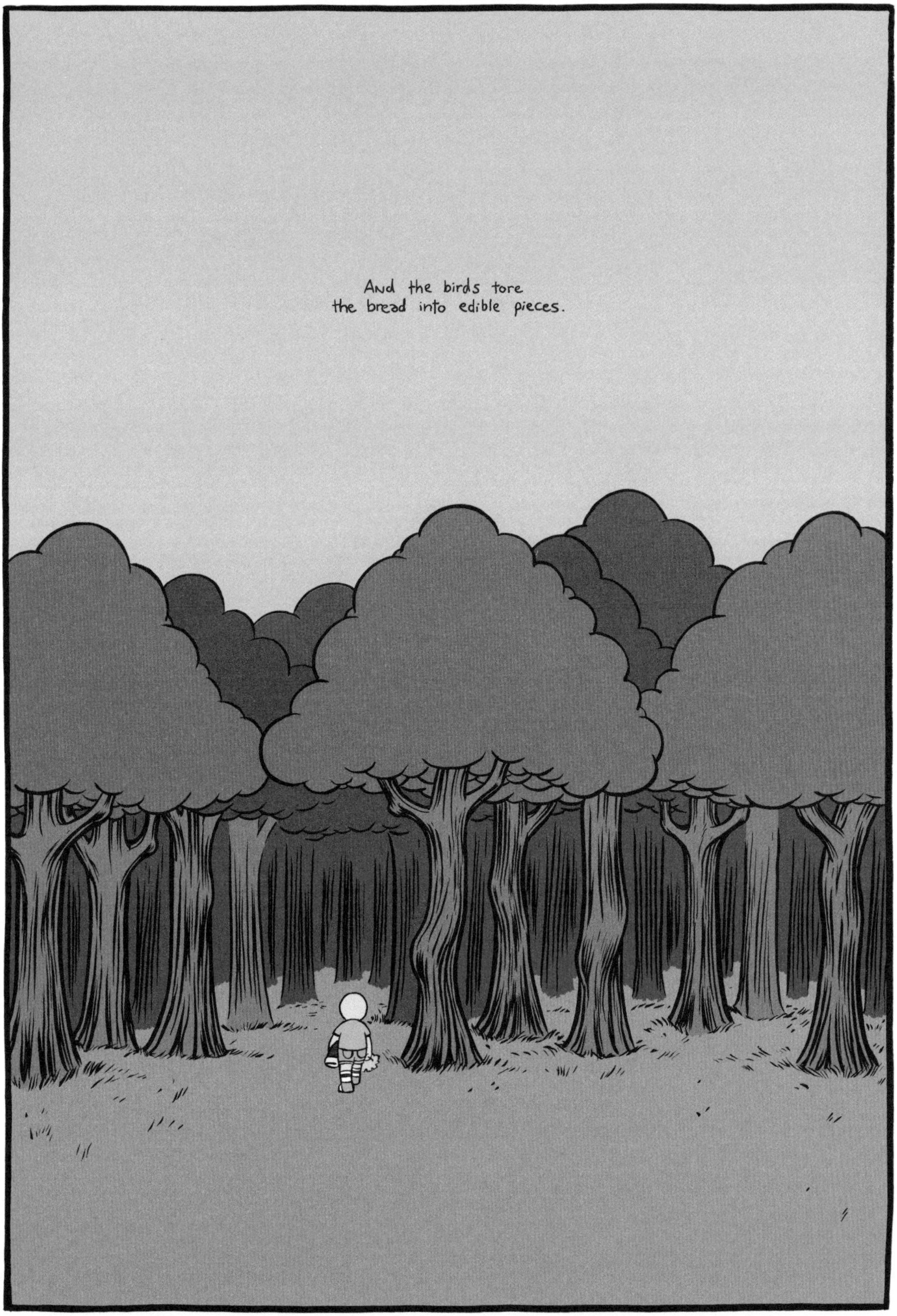
And the birds tore
the bread into edible pieces.

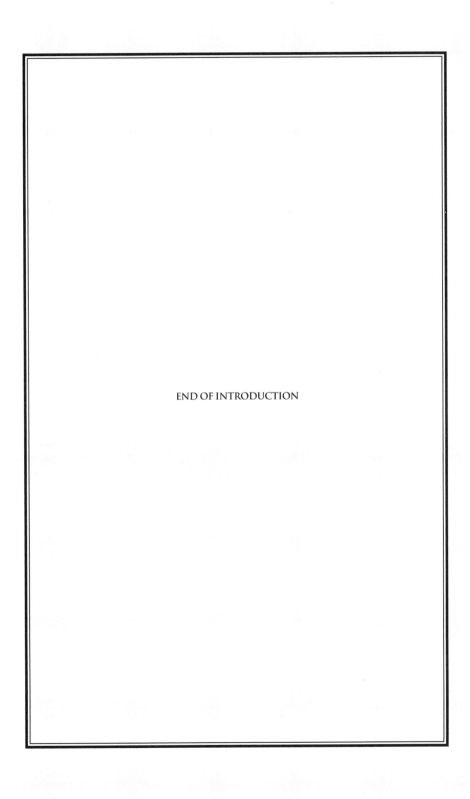

END OF INTRODUCTION

CHAPTER ONE

"WE ARE ALL RELEASED"

MANY THANKS

There are many who have suffered needlessly,
or given generously, or some combination
thereof, during the production of this book.
They are thanked here, inadequately, by listing
their names: Patrick Hornschemeier, Margaret
Clark, Ann and Eric Cardiff, Mary and Dan
Bandstra, Diana Schutz, Ed Irvin, Kathleen
Kranack, Professor Neil Tennant, Josh Farkas,
Jeffrey Brown, Anders Nilsen, John Hankiewicz,
Bo Altes, Mat Biscan, Dan Hyatt, Lisa Jaronski,
Chelsea Hilton, Farel Dalrymple, Chris Young,
Will Eisner, Frank Miller, Craig Thompson,
Nick Bertozzi, Chris Ware, Dan Raeburn,
Erynn Wheatley, Michelle Patterson, Dwight
Dyer, Sammy Harkham, Chris Pitzer, Brett
Warnock, Tomer Hanuka, Tom Herpich,
James Jean, Richard Hahn, Kelli Flanery,
Daniel Bishop, Cheryl Weaver, Juliane Graf,
Jay Ryan, Postergirl Press, Henry Owings,
Quimby's Bookstore, and Emily Eirich.
Thank you to all cartoonists whose conversations
helped urge this collection forward, all readers
and letter writers who made the pursuit
worthwhile, and immeasurable thanks to
Tchaikovsky and Sigur Ros, to whose music
most of this collection was drawn.

Original art from this and other works by
the author are available through:

Charles A. Hartman Fine Art
www.hartmanfineart.net

For information and missives, please visit:

newsandheadlice.blogspot.com
or forlornfunnies.com

Or to contact the author :
thomas@forlornfunnies.com

ABOUT THE AUTHOR

PAUL HORNSCHEMEIER was born in Cincinnati in 1977 and was reared in rural Georgetown, Ohio. While attending college, he began publishing his experimental comics series, *Sequential*. Upon moving to Chicago, he began the series *Forlorn Funnies*, from which *Mother, Come Home* was cultivated. He currently resides in Chicago with his cat Margo, producing *Forlorn Funnies* and myriad other comics and stories.

GALLERY

PROMOTIONAL ARTWORK
FROM THE FIRST EDITION

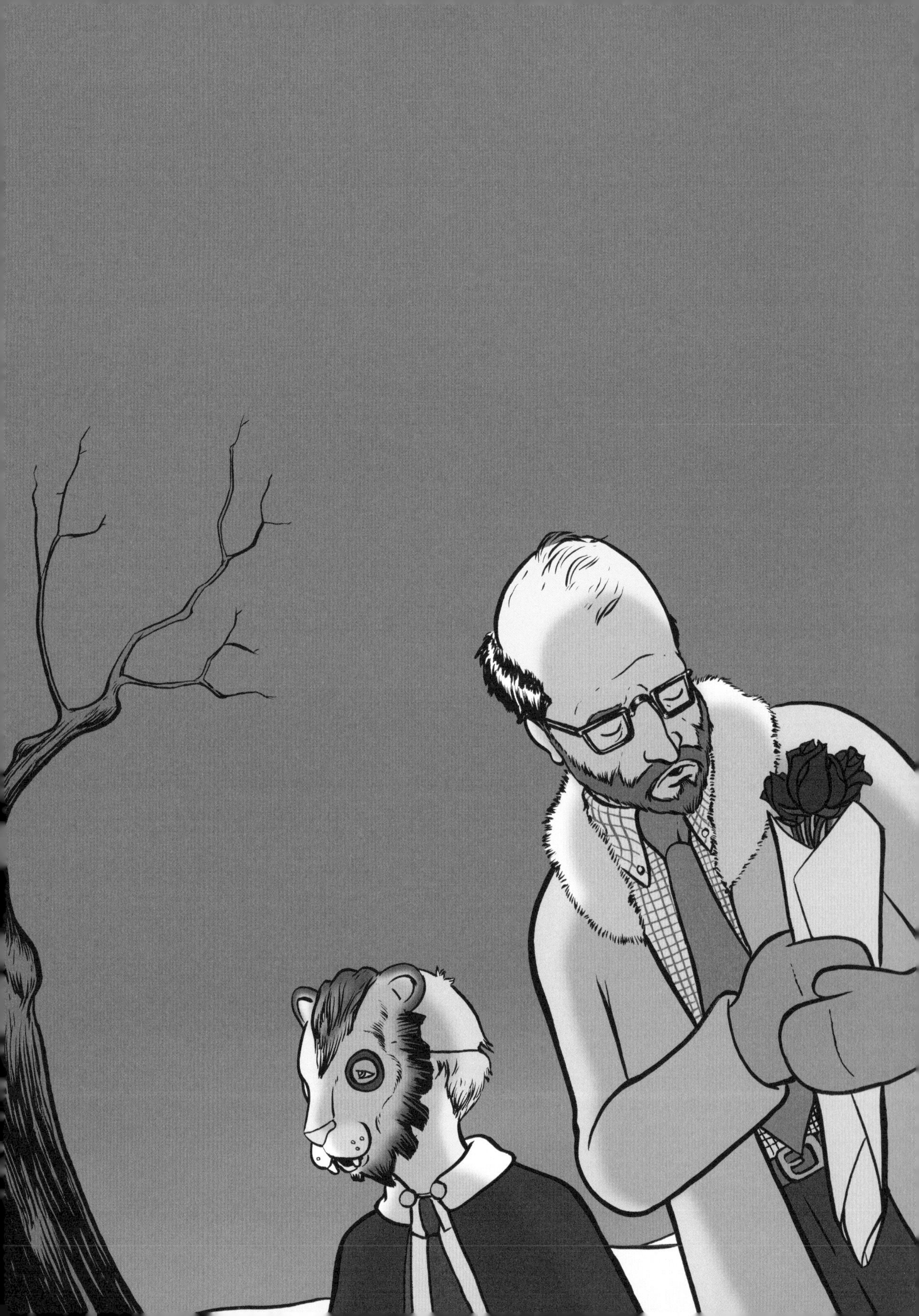

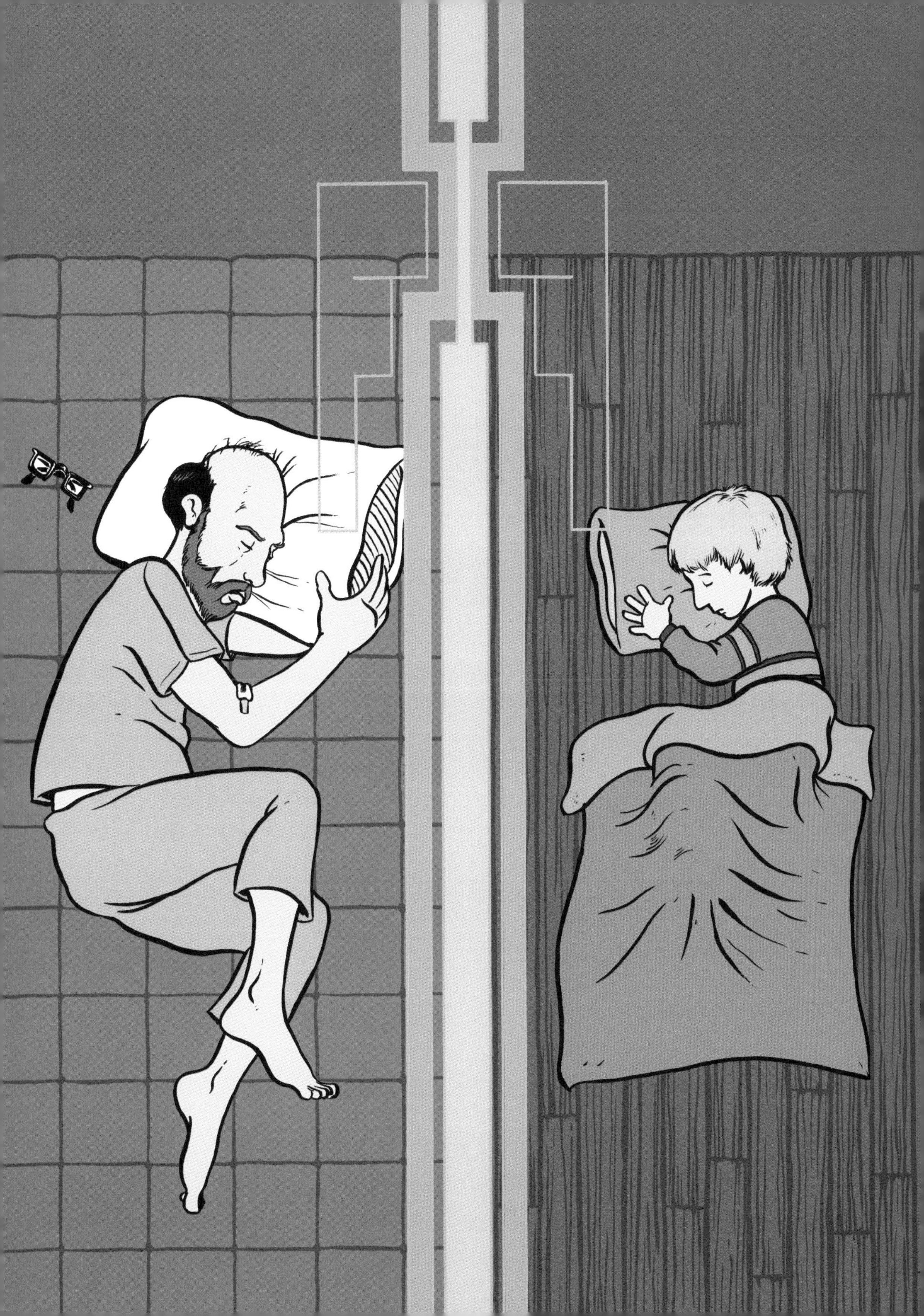

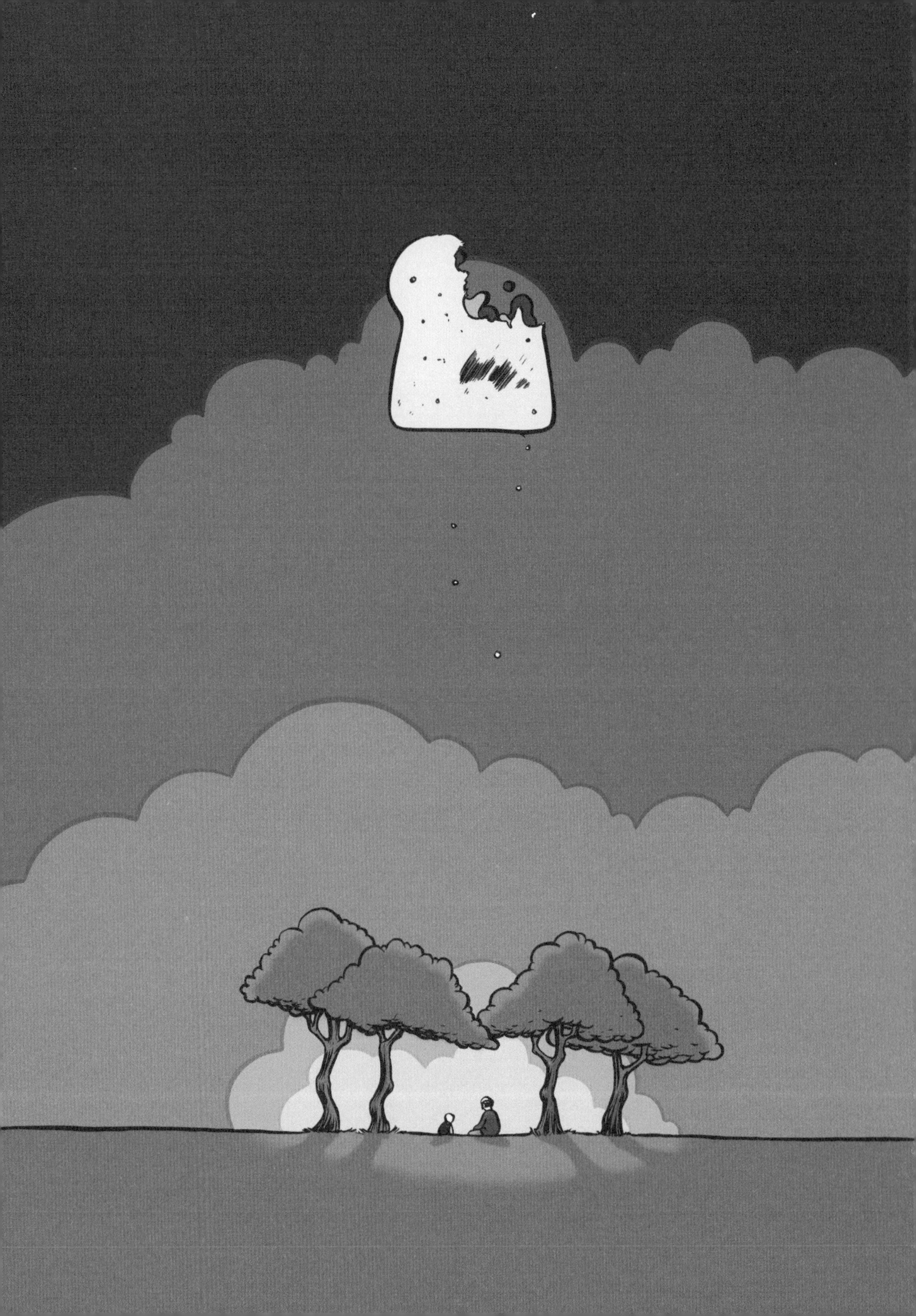

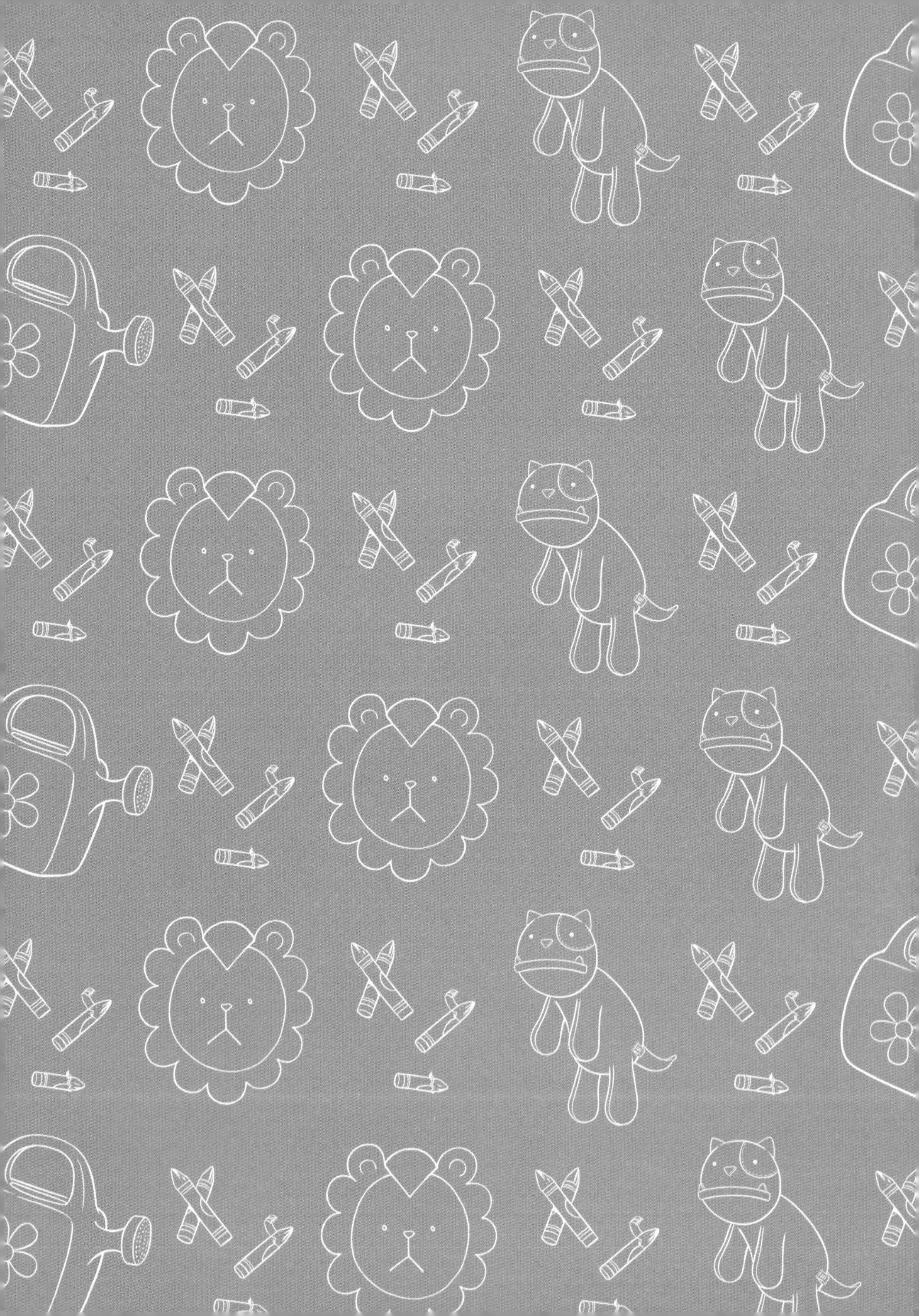